RV Living for Beginners

2019

Live Your Dream with RV Retirement Living

Prep Guide to Full-Time RV Living

ADAM THOMPSON

© Copyright 2019 Adam Thompson - All rights reserved.

The content contained within this book may not be reproduced, duplicated or transmitted without direct written permission from the author or the publisher.

Under no circumstances will any blame or legal responsibility be held against the publisher, or author, for any damages, reparation, or monetary loss due to the information contained within this book. Either directly or indirectly.

Legal Notice:

This book is copyright protected. This book is only for personal use. You cannot amend, distribute, sell, use, quote or paraphrase any part, or the content within this book, without the consent of the author or publisher.

Disclaimer Notice:

Please note the information contained within this document is for educational and entertainment purposes only. All effort has been executed to present accurate, up to date, and reliable, complete information. No warranties of any kind are declared or implied. Readers acknowledge that the author is not engaging in the rendering of legal, financial, medical or professional advice. The content within this book has been derived from various sources. Please consult a licensed professional before attempting any techniques outlined in this book.

By reading this document, the reader agrees that under no circumstances is the author responsible for any losses, direct or indirect, which are incurred as a result of the use of information contained within this document, including, but not limited to, — errors, omissions, or inaccuracies.

TABLE OF CONTENTS

INTRODUCTION 1

CHAPTER 1: THE RV LIFESTYLE 3
    RV – WHAT IS IT? 3
    THE RV LIFESTYLE 4
    WHAT ARE THE BENEFITS OF THE RV LIFESTYLE FOR YOUR KIDS? 10
    OTHER BENEFITS OF THE RV LIFESTYLE 13

CHAPTER 2- FINDING THE RIGHT RV 15
    FEATURES OF RV'S TO CONSIDER 15
    CHOOSING THE RIGHT RV 19
    OTHER CONSIDERATIONS 28
    SHOULD YOU PURCHASE NEW OR USED? 30
    SHOULD YOU RENT RATHER THAN BUY ONE? 31
    RENT FROM A REPUTABLE RV DEALER 31
    IS SHARING A BETTER CHOICE? 32

CHAPTER 3- HOW TO TAKE THE LEAP AND TRANSITION INTO THE RV LIFESTYLE 34
    RV GPS 34
    GETTING INTERNET ACCESS ON YOUR RV 37

RV DRIVER LICENSE REQUIREMENTS 42

HOW TO GET YOUR MAIL WHILE ON THE ROAD 45

GETTING PACKAGES WHILE ON THE ROAD 50

RV INSURANCE – WHAT KIND OF INSURANCE DO YOU NEED FOR YOUR RV? 50

OTHER FORMS OF INSURANCE FOR THE RV OWNER & HIS FAMILY 55

CHAPTER 4- PREPPING TIPS TO GET STARTED FULL TIME 57

RV TANKS- WHAT KIND OF TANKS DO YOU NEED FOR YOUR RV? 57

RV JACKS – WHY DO YOU NEED ONE? 63

RV PACKING TIPS FOR NEWBIES 66

THINGS TO DO BEFORE LEAVING 68

MEETING YOUR POWER REQUIREMENTS ON THE ROAD 72

RV DRIVING TIPS 77

CHAPTER 5 - FINANCIAL PREPARATIONS 81

IMPORTANT FINANCIAL PREPARATIONS 81

FINANCIAL PREPARATIONS FOR A TOWED VEHICLE 85

CAMPGROUNDS 86

FINANCIAL PLAN FOR FOOD 88

INSURANCE 89

MAIL SERVICE 90

LAUNDRY 90

CLOTHING 90

ELECTRONICS 91

PETS 92

ENTERTAINMENT 92

SAVINGS 92

OTHER SAVINGS GOALS 94

MONTHLY FINANCIAL PLAN SAMPLE 94

CHAPTER 6- EARNING INCOME WHILE ON THE ROAD 96

DO SOME PLANNING AND PREPARATION 97

JOBS ON THE MOVE 97

RENTING OUT YOUR PROPERTIES 104

MAKING MONEY ONLINE 105

CHAPTER 7 - GUIDE TO LIVING COMFORTABLE IN AN RV 113

EATING HEALTHILY – HOW TO EAT HEALTHILY WHILE ON THE ROAD 114

EXERCISING AND STAYING FIT 117

KEEPING WARM ON THE ROAD 120

KEEPING YOUR RV COOL 124

KEEPING YOUR RV TIDY 127

v

COOKING – HOW TO COOK MEALS IN AN RV 129

DISHWARE 132

KEEPING THE RV CLEAN 133

CHAPTER 8: LIFE ON THE ROAD AND MUST VISIT DESTINATIONS FOR US RV TRAVELERS 140

RV PARKS, CAMPGROUNDS, AND TRAILER PARKS; HOW ARE THEY DIFFERENT? 140

FREE RV CAMPGROUNDS AND CAMPING 142

MAINTAINING YOUR RV – WHY YOU SHOULD CREATE A MONTHLY CHECKLIST 145

QUARTERLY CHECKLIST FOR MAINTENANCE – WHAT SHOULD IT ENTAIL? 147

RV MEMBERSHIPS AND CLUBS 151

PLACES YOU MUST CHECK OUT IF YOU ARE IN THE US 153

MUST VISIT DESTINATIONS FOR US TRAVELERS: LONGER RV ROAD TRIPS 156

CONCLUSION 159

INTRODUCTION

Many people have fantasized about leaving everything behind and enjoying the freedom that comes with an RV lifestyle. Some have tried without really arming themselves with the appropriate information and have ended up backing out and leaving this dream behind.

Others have succeeded in making this dream a reality. So, why did some succeed, while others didn't? Well, that is what we will be discussing in this book.

If you are thinking of going into RVing full time, you need to ensure you are adequately prepared. This will ensure that chasing your dream is not terrifying when you are nowhere close to home.

If you want to make your RV dream a reality, this book is for you. The book comes with useful advice about life on the road. It provides you with an idea of what you need to know about RVing full-time. This book covers everything from transitioning to a standard home to the full-time/part-time RV lifestyle.

I do not promise you that everything will be smooth, without any hitches, as RVing also comes with its own hassles. However, I promise you that by the time you are done reading this book, you will have in-depth knowledge on the RV lifestyle. Also, if you do apply the information in this book, you will be sure to have a more seamless transition into the RV lifestyle.

Future RVer, follow me as we take a more in-depth look into the RV lifestyle.

CHAPTER 1:
THE RV LIFESTYLE

RV – What is it?

I am going to assume that you at least know exactly what an RV is, but if you do not, the following definition can come in handy.

An RV is a recreational vehicle. It is a trailer or motor vehicle which consists of a living space that is ideal for accommodation. RVs come in various types including campervans, motorhomes, truck campers, fifth-wheel trailers, and others. We will be taking a more extensive look at these later on in the book.

Now that we have this covered, let's take a look at what the RV lifestyle is all about.

The RV lifestyle

Many people typically think that RVing is for retirees who have saved for ages to be able to live in an RV full-time. Although a considerable portion of RVers consists of retirees, families, and individuals from all walks of life are getting into the RV lifestyle.

Many people have left their homes and some have sold it all in a bid to live in an RV full time.

Regardless of if you are 20 or 70, have a full-time job or are a retiree, there are others like you out there enjoying the RV lifestyle.

The RV lifestyle is filled with so much fun and excitement. Also, there is a tremendous amount of freedom that comes with it. There is this thrill you feel knowing that you can take time off anytime you want. These are just a few of the benefits you stand to gain from getting into the RV lifestyle.

If you are still skeptical about becoming a part of the RV lifestyle, the following are a few reasons why you shouldn't.

Insane amount of Freedom!

This is one of the most obvious reasons to get into full-time RVing. When you sign a lease on a home, what it implies is that you are going to remain in that same environment for the length of the contract.

However, those living in an RV full-time have the flexibility to pick up their things and move whenever they desire. If a new temporary job opportunity shows up in a different part of the country, they will be able to pack up their homes and head to the new location.

Also, it's the same case if there is an emergency where you need to be present or if a member of your family gets ill and needs you to take care of them. Nothing ties you down if you want to move. You don't need to book flights or make comprehensive plans, and you don't need to ensure your cat or dog will be fine.

You can get up one morning and decide you want to head to Australia or the Pacific coastline and nothing will stop you. In minutes, you are ready and, on your way, to experiencing something new.

RVing also implies that you have the freedom to select the climate of your choice. If Florida is not as hot as you would like, you can head to Arizona. You can head to any location to accommodate your needs.

Meet New People

Many RVers who are in it full-time tend to pick a campground or RV resort as their home. These provide them with opportunities to lease for a long time. Many such locations offer pools, amenities, fitness centers, and clubhouses, among other activities.

These activities and events will allow you to meet many likeminded people who have decided to be on the road full-time. You will find a sense of fun and community. In this kind of places, you might even get to make some friends that will last a lifetime.

There is a range of communities that can bring you closer to other RVers like yourself.

Live a more fulfilling life

Another reason to go full-time RVing is that the quality of life it offers is much better than average. Individuals RVing full-time are likely to benefit from the great outdoors, have more activities, and live a healthier lifestyle.

All these factors have been proven to contribute to the quality of life and happiness. Aside from that, many people who have RVed with one another have reported that they grew more powerful bonds and relationships as a result of their lifestyle.

RVing full time gives you an opportunity to escape from everything and see the country how you desire. You will be able to come and leave as you want which can offer you relaxation, comfort, and adventure at the same time. The RV lifestyle puts you in charge of where and how you want your life to be.

The RV Lifestyle Is Budget Friendly

Another reason to go with the RV lifestyle is that traveling in an RV is not as expensive as traveling in other ways. Travelers who use their RVs to go on trips save lots of money by not buying pricey hotel rooms, flights, and restaurant meals.

Individuals who travel full-time have the chance to live in a space that is much more affordable than staying in a typical home. When you are living on the road, even your utility costs go down drastically.

The RV Lifestyle Is Simple

Staying at home can be stressful, but it is relaxing to stay on the road. The RV lifestyle pushes you to live in an enclosed space with those you cherish.

In an RV, you have limited belongings, and you maximize the time you spend with loved ones. Leaving the busy daily life behind helps everyone create memories together and relax.

No More Yard work with the RV lifestyle

One of the best aspects of not staying in a traditional home is that you save lots of time in routine things that come along with living in a typical house.

These include monthly bills like; water, trash, etc. Living In an RV, you are only restricted to a few fees whenever you head to a new location.

Although RVs are not flawless, you do not spend as much in an RV as you would in a house. This means you won't have to do things like mow the grass, rake leaves, etc.

It is liberating to downsize

Living in an RV implies that you will need to downsize. While some people do not look forward to this, eradicating almost everything you own can offer you liberation.

You will also need to be more mindful of what you purchase, and you will not waste your resources. Also, when you are living the RV lifestyle, you don't need to purchase as many things because you spend more time outdoors.

Instead of heading to stores, you will spend a lot of time checking out new locations.

RV living implies you can move if you don't fancy your neighbors

It's likely that you have once resided next to a neighbor you were uncomfortable with. The great aspect about the RV lifestyle is if you have an annoying neighbor or anyone you do not get along with, all you need to do is move your home!!

You can work and travel at the same time.

Yes, it is possible to do both. For some people, this may be scary to think of, but it is a possibility that can let you live the life of your dreams.

There are many jobs you can do, even if you are living in your RV full-time. Also, you will be able to make a reasonable amount of cash from any location while living the life of your dreams.

This is a factor that stops many potential RVers from getting into it, but don't let it discourage you, as there is always a way to work around this situation.

Increase your savings

Imagine having the capacity to head to the location of your choice without having to pay for rental cars, airfare, and lodging. Also, RV parks, which have many features are not as expensive as traveling conventionally.

This will allow you to further invest in your travel savings.

Spend more time with family

Another reason to RV is because you will be traveling with family and spending more time with those you care about. It typically takes you away from the distractions that prevent you from spending quality time with your family.

What are the Benefits of the RV lifestyle for your kids?

Many families want to leave the world behind and tour the country in an RV, but they are not sure that it is a great idea to go with their kids and live in an RV full-time. Questions arise; for example, how will the kids feel about leaving everything behind? How will they go to school on the road?

But in reality, RVing with the children is an excellent chance for the entire family. There are a range of benefits for your kids that they would be unable to get from other experiences which is the case even if you are RVing part-time for many months.

The following are life lessons your kids can learn from RVing.

What beauty and nature are like in reality

Although documentaries can paint a picture in the mind of your child about how wonderful nature is; it is nothing like real life.

Irrespective of if you are living in an RV full-time or just taking a lengthy vacation, your kids will have firsthand experience of nature and grandeur.

RV adventures offer your kids the chance to check out the numerous wonders of creation and to see different landscapes from various regions.

How they can live with less

No one wants their kids to be spoiled with material things. One of the main benefits of living an RV lifestyle with kids is that it teaches them how to survive with less. As you make plans to move into your RV, you can help your kids consider the belongings that are crucial to them, and what they can keep in storage.

After being on the road for a while, take time to speak about the items they left behind and how they have survived without them. Help them think about the things that are important for them to be happy.

The RV lifestyle offers new opportunities

Every time you go on an RV trip, you come across new places, adventures and individuals; the RV Lifestyle helps keep life interesting by presenting adults and kids with new experiences daily.

You may believe that traveling in an RV will broaden your horizon, and there is no doubt that it will broaden your kid's too.

How to be a family

The traditional family calendar is filled with activities, and members of the family are spread out as every person is headed in a different direction, to things like networking meetups, sports activities, youth groups, etc. Everyone has a diverse schedule that takes a chunk of their family time away.

RVing ensures you get your quality family time back, and allows you to know the members of your family on a deeper level.

RVing with your kids also teaches the members of your family how they can better live together. When you are in a small space and spend almost no time apart from one another, you will quickly understand how crucial it is to learn to get along.

As a family, becoming part of the RV lifestyle teaches you how to overlook the little stuff, how to be patient, and how to function as a family in creative ways.

You will find out new ways of relating and different kinds of innovative solutions which will all help you to enrich your relationships.

How to meet new people and accept them

While traveling and living on the road for a long time, your kids will make many new friends. For some kids, it will take time to get used to, especially if they are not the social, outgoing type.

However, it will amaze you to see how their capacity to make new friends with individuals who are very different from them will grow. They will attain confidence around new individuals and learn how to easily connect with others.

That learning can occur anywhere

Road schooling or homeschooling on the road offers your family a precious and rare chance to experiment in a way that hands-on education and textbooks do not offer.

There are amazing criteria for homeschooling available for families in the RV lifestyle. Locate one you like and fill it up with your family experiences.

For example, you can visit museums and nature centers or exploit junior ranger programs at national parks. Check out the historical places your kids only see in textbooks. Study the solar system and explore nature. There is no better education than firsthand experience.

Other Benefits of the RV lifestyle

There is a multitude of other benefits you stand to gain when living in an RV full-time. The major ones are those we have discussed above.

Just like everything else, RVing full-time does not suit everyone. If you are uncertain if it is appropriate or you, you may want to try it out for a few weeks and see how you feel when you get back home.

Drive more than you ever have, visit locations that you never thought you would and find locations for dry camping, so you have a feel of the various aspects of RVing. From there, you can determine if living like this full-time is the right choice for you.

CHAPTER 2-
FINDING THE RIGHT RV

It is a dream for many individuals to travel in their own personal RV. Having the chance to simply drive and stop in various locations to visit is the best way to discover the country.

However, before you go purchasing the first RV you find, there are many things you should first consider. This is even more applicable if you have never driven or owned one.

If you plan to buy an RV, the following factors can help you find the best RV for your needs.

Features of RV's to Consider

The needs of all individuals differ, so it may take you some time to look through various RVs to find the ideal one for you.

There is a saying that you begin searching for your next RV the moment you buy the initial one. This is because as you start to use it, you will quickly understand what is suitable and what isn't for you and your family.

The following are core features of an RV that you should consider before you buy.

Beds – Type and Number

Many people's first thought is regarding the RV's sleeping arrangement. The style and number of beds will depend on what you require. Some individuals choose to go with a bed that does not move, so they won't need to make it up every night before they sleep. However, some don't mind converting the bed daily. Some individuals even choose to have a distinct bedroom in the RV.

Also, some beds come with bunks, while some are foldable, depending on your needs.

Seating: Size, Arrangement, and Kinds

The seating arrangement is absolutely crucial in your RV, and it is hugely dependent on your circumstances. Consider the number of individuals you will be traveling with and if you plan on entertaining them in your RV.

Many RVs also come with some form of dining area, so ensure it will comfortably fit your whole family. Also, tables are usually foldable in order to get additional space when you are not making use of it.

It is crucial to be able to relax and to feel at home in your RV.

Kitchens – Storage and Appliances

The majority of RV kitchens come with some form of sink, cooking appliance and fridge. Of course, kitchen appliances and sizes will increase depending on the size of the RV.

So, in many small RVs, you have small kitchen appliances and areas while in larger RVs, you will find more grand and luxurious sizes. Also, many modern RVs come with microwaves.

Your oven and stove will run on gas. Refrigerators often run on both electricity and gas, and in modern RVs, the system will switch back and forth as needed.

Another thing to note is your storage space. Consider the number of cups, mugs, cutlery, cutting boards, coffee pots, pans, and other utensils that you may need to purchase. All of these little items add up, and it is an excellent idea to have an area where you can securely store and organize them.

Bathrooms

Very few trailers or RVs come without a bathroom. In little RVs, it might just be a wet bath which is in a small enclosed room. Here, you can both sit on the toilet and have your shower simultaneously. The benefit is that it does not take much space. The drawback is that it is not spacious and everything in the room can get wet.

Bigger RVs come with better-sized bathrooms, equipped with sinks, toilets and showers or bathtubs. Therefore, it is crucial to consider the kind of bathroom you would like and try it out when shopping for an RV.

Entertainment Systems

Many RVs come with stereo systems and a way to hook up a television. Older RVs often come with large TVs while a majority of the recent ones come with flat-screen TVs to save space. Consider where the TV is mounted and if it can move around or not. Also, you need to be sure you can see it correctly from your ideal sitting spot.

Recent RVs even have external entertainment systems, which allows you to sit outside your RV door and relax with your entertainment system, and this is ideal for when you're entertaining guests.

Slide-Outs:

Slide-outs are great features as it allows RV walls to be able to slide out when you park. This lengthens the internal part of the RV. Slide outs are ideal for adding size to your RV, which is an excellent choice if you have a huge family.

You need to understand that the slides will make your rig heavier, so you need to park in locations with adequate space to slide them out.

Choosing the right RV

When deciding on the ideal RV, it is easy to get confused due to the variety of classes and options available. The trick is to understand your budget, do comprehensive research and have the perfect idea on where you want to travel and who will be traveling with you.

Below is an outline of the various types and kinds of motorhomes and RVs that are available to you. We will also outline the advantages and drawback of each option to make it easy to find the right RV for you and your family.

Motorhomes

Nothing beats the delight of RV camping, but not everyone has similar goals and needs, so it is crucial to go with a vehicle that fits your budget and expectations. Motorhomes come with many more benefits than travel trailer versions of RVs.

They are usually totally self-contained, less difficult to set up at campsites, and have space for other occupants to move around.

There are three kinds of motorhomes you can pick from. The following are the benefits and drawbacks of the three classes of motorhomes you can choose from.

Class A

These are the largest and costliest RVs on the road, and the preferred option for more dedicated travelers. Variants consist of purpose-built models and converted buses. You can set up the driveline as puller or pusher configurations and run either by a gasoline or diesel engine. Although some of these are as long as 45 feet, you do not need a special CDL license to operate one legally.

These motorhomes provide the most features and interior space. Some come with slide-out areas that increase the living quarters, and it is not uncommon to have a distinct master bedroom suite. The range of amenities, appliances, and features are limitless.

Popular perks consist of ice makers, shower facilities, driers, laundry machines, and amazing home entertainment systems. They also come with lots of basement storage for your belongings. Campers will be able to store adequate resources in their RVs, which will allow them to be on the road for a long time.

Although these are fantastic options for full-time camping and weekend getaways, they are costly, and for many people, their size is intimidating. With motorhomes, you will be unable to access certain narrow routes. Also, parking in secluded camping sites may also be an issue with this vehicle. In addition, it might be a hassle to simply run a quick errand once you have set up in a location.

Also, aside from how expensive it is, the fuel, insurance, and repair costs are also expensive comparing to other motorhomes. These may be impractical for many people, but they are great options for retirees and individuals who have an interest in living on the road full-time.

Class B

This class is often called the Camper Van. It consists of many smaller vehicles that you can barely classify as motorhomes. They are developed on a standard complete sized van and come with a roof which is raised to enable you to walk upright. Similarly to the Class A, there are both gasoline and diesel variants of this vehicle.

These campers offer their occupants comfortable sleeping quarters and all other life necessities. As a result of their little size, you can easily maneuver, drive and store them. You can also take these on a quick trip or run errands. These vehicles can accommodate one or two people with ease and are usually completely self-contained. Campers will be able to take advantage of access to heating and AC, hot water, toilets, showers, refrigerators, among others.

Although you would initially have to invest a substantial amount of cash to purchase this vehicle, it is not that expensive to operate. These versions come with cramped interior spaces and if more than one traveler is going to be using it, the non-spacious quarters can quickly get uncomfortable.

The appliance sizes are also not as large as many need them to be. It does not have enough space for luxuries such as full-size entertainment systems or laundry facilities. It also does not have ample cargo space to carry supplies.

Individuals traveling by themselves or those without kids will be able to enjoy the convenience and affordability of this kind of motorhome. They are also the best choice for those who are still employed and only have time to take occasional trips.

Class C

These are mid-sized RVs which fall between 20 to 33 feet in size. They are constructed above a van chassis and existing truck. They are meant for larger groups or families that want to go on a vacation on a restricted budget. These options come with many of the same considerations and benefits of class A motorhomes, but at a reduced cost.

These versions provide a much larger living space than class B. Also, it comes with a lot of similar facilities to class A motorhomes. They usually come with a shower and a toilet, a great kitchen and many different places to sleep.

Some of the bigger models come with a master bedroom at the back. Tables and couches convert into beds and the section above the cab can be utilized to store belongings. They can also be used as extra sleeping quarters. Because of the compartmental construction of the cab, you can easily get in via the side doors.

These motorhomes can be as difficult to drive as Class A ones; however, you can easily manage them in campsites with more restrictions. Most travelers often tow another vehicle to use for errands and excursions. It comes with a slightly better fuel cost as well as insurance and maintenance. Nonetheless, they are still a little costly to operate comparing to those of Class B.

These are a great option for families with kids traveling on a restricted budget. They offer all the basic aspects of RV camping and traveling that all RVers love.

Towable RVs

When choosing the kind of RV that is suitable for you, it is crucial to balance its functionalities and costs with your goals and requirements. These RVs provide lots of benefits over full motorhomes. They do not cost as much to purchase and are more reliable. They also offer the comfort of a detachable vehicle which you can use to run errands and explore.

Before you make your choice, you need to consider the different options available in the market. Let's have a look at some of them below:

Travel Trailers

Travel trailers are huge portable containers packed with living spaces and all the comfort of a home. They are developed above the standard frame of a trailer and come fitted with a host of facilities.

You have the choice to leave it simple or fill it up with all kinds of luxuries you can think of. Many come with bathrooms, small refrigerators, kitchens, and water supplies. Sizes can be drastically different, and some of them come with expandable areas to offer campers a more internal space to relax.

The main benefits of a standard travel trailer are the range of towing vehicles you can use with it as they link with a normal ball hitch receiver. You can also pull them using an SUV, van or truck with the appropriate rating to deal with the weight, so you don't need to buy a different vehicle to service any specific needs.

Similar to all trailers, it is not easy to maneuver, as driving in reverse while it is linked is almost impossible. For individuals who have rear extended living quarters, tail swing becomes a problem when driving. Also, it is crucial that trailers are level and it can be a hassle to remove and set up the tow vehicle.

A travel trailer system may be a great option for fulltime campers and little families, depending on their budget.

5th Wheel Trailers

5th wheel trailers share lots of similarities with normal travel trailers, with one core exception - they come with a gooseneck connector which links to the tow vehicle. This comes with a host of benefits and few restrictions.

Towing the vehicle is not complex; the gooseneck stretches past the rear of the towing truck and attaches beneath an overhanging area of the trailer. There is additional leverage from the middle of the truck to ensure it is easier to maneuver.

The overhanging area of the trailer also provides extra internal space which you won't find in the normal travel trailer. These connections are much easier and stronger to manage than standard ball hitches.

The greatest issue with these trailers is the kind of vehicle you must use for towing. It is necessary to have a truck that has a flat or open bed, which can be an issue for huge families as there is limited space for passengers.

It is not legal for anyone to be in a vehicle being towed. Also, these types of vehicles may not be great to check out surrounding environments compared to other SUVs or passenger vans.

The cost, flexibility, and dependability of these styles make them the ideal option for lots of serious RVers.

Folding and Tent Trailers

Folding and tent trailers are some of the smallest towable RVs you can find. They come with a collapsible section which minimizes their outer profiles and makes them less difficult to store when idle. Some are constructed using study composite walls which fold down and others are made from long-lasting tent canvas.

These trailers are ideal for occasional camping adventures as they are not heavy, you can maneuver them with ease, and they come with lots of towing options. Station wagons, little trucks and full-sized sedans fitted with the proper ball hitch receivers can be used to haul these RVs. They provide you with the bare survival essentials and ensure camping is more convenient.

Because of how they are designed, it is hard to store things in them, so you need to carry equipment and supplies separately. The canvas areas and folding joints easily wear out and may eventually be subject to leaks.

Other core necessities, like kitchen facilities and toilets are often small or even absent. These are normally a great option for starters and make excellent part-time camping vehicles.

Toy Hauler/Sports Utility RV Trailers

Toy haulers merge the features of a sports utility trailer with a travel RV trailer. They are ideal for individuals who want to bring their dirt bikes, snow bikes or ATVs with them. The rear section is utilized for the storage of a sports vehicle and comes with a folding wall which also functions as a loading ramp. Forward compartments come with living areas for campers.

Outdoor lovers who want to partake in motorsports while camping usually choose these kinds of towable RVs. They provide many of the same basic features as the more costly travel trailers.

The major drawback of these trailers is the inadequate living quarters inside. While towing a full-sized trailer may be required, only a part of the internal space is significant to campers. Also, some may not like staying close to supplies and motorized equipment, and fuel, oil, along with other chemicals may lead to pungent smells and other hazards to the environment.

A Sports Utility RV trailer is ideal for active outdoor lovers. They provide many of the necessities that leave campers adequately rested and comfortable between adventures.

So, which RV suits you best? It's down to you to choose the vehicle that best suits your requirements.

Other considerations

How do you Plan on utilizing your RV?

To help select the best RV for you, identify how you plan to use it.

Consider the following:

- **What do you plan on utilizing the RV for?**

    A Good RV for weekend trips may not be suitable to live full-time in. It is very important you consider this so that you don't end up with the wrong kind of RV.

- **Who will you be going with?**

    This is also essential. It is crucial to consider those you plan on RVing with before you make your choice. Will it just be you or will you be with family members? Do you have pets? All these questions will help you in choosing the right one.

- **Write down a list of your best RV features.**

    This list should assist you in making your selection. Note the features that are important to you and those that are not. Also, you can update your RV to include features you need over time, so be ready to consider this.

- **Where you plan on staying should matter**

    Do you plan on staying in warmer areas? If yes, purchase an RV fitted with an AC, and fans are also helpful. If you plan to head to colder climates, you want to ensure that the RV you are purchasing comes with a great heating system or furnace.

How frequently do you plan on using your RV?

- **Part-time or Full-time?**

    How frequently you will utilize your RV will also help in determining the best option for you.

- **Your lifestyle matters**

    Individuals who have recently retired will probably have lots of time to enjoy fully RVing. However, busy entrepreneurs who need to be around their office may not have this luxury.

    This is one of the main factors that individuals base their whole purchasing decision on.

Should you purchase new or used?

Many people battle with the process of picking the appropriate RV. Aside from choosing between the various classes of RVs, prospective RVers also need to determine their budget and decide whether to purchase a new or used one.

A new RV will come with the most recent features. Also, it won't have any mileage. A used RV, on the other hand, will come at a reduced cost but with mileage and use from the past owner.

Prices of a new RV may vary and are subject to local market conditions, extra dealer fees, and chosen facilities. Average RV costs fall around the range of $40,000 and above, but fifth wheels and high-end RVs can cost as high as $75,000 and above. New motorized RVs with a range of amenities can cost more than $1 million.

If you're on a budget, you can minimize your cost by looking at the used RV market.

Prices tend to fluctuate a lot, so it's ideal you check out a recent source like NADA Guides to verify the present market value. Use the website in your search for new and used RVs to make sure you are getting a great deal.

Purchasing a used RV is a great way to get the all the features you like at a reduced price.

Should you rent rather than buy one?

If you are on an even tighter budget, you can save a lot by renting RVs instead. Also, short-term rentals allow you to test out a host of models before buying one.

Ultimately, RVers who spend lots of time on the road in a rental have a better chance of picking the RV they desire. Using the experienced they gained in rental RVs, they will have the ability to determine the size, type, and features that best fit their needs.

Individuals who frequently rent RVs will also learn that the renting fees will continuously rise, so in the long-term, purchasing one will allow you to reduce costs. However, the huge amount of funds required as well as possible costs of ownership and installment payments makes renting a better choice for some.

The decision to keep renting or to buy an RV will ultimately depend on your budget and how you plan on utilizing it.

Rent from a reputable RV dealer

If you're RVing on a budget, renting is the way to go. When you rent an RV, be prepared to pay roughly $1,000-$1,200 per week for a 25-foot class C motorhome with a lot of mileage. Motorhome rentals typically come fully equipped with kitchen utensils, plates, glasses, cups, cooking pots, towels, and bedding, so leave those items at home!

Opt for trusty RV dealers to ensure you're renting a well-maintained vehicle suited to your trip, all while paying a competitive price. Ask the dealer as many questions as possible to make sure you get the best RV for your needs. This way, you'll have access to great RV travel tips regarding how to use the vehicle safely, which routes to take, the best campsites and even suggested meals.

Is sharing a better choice?

RV sharing is a similar idea to Airbnb, which has become the largest hotel chain in the world without even owning a hotel. New websites like Outdoorsy have been created to meet RVers' needs.

This is a seamless method of starting in the RV world without having to use up all your resources. It also saves you from the expenses and stress of owning an RV for a long time.

Because the concept of RV sharing is still quite new, it is crucial to be cautious when checking out these websites. Do not be drawn in by reward programs and other incentives that they may offer. Instead, search for organizations that provide insurance for the renter and owner, appropriate DMV screening, and roadside support like Outdoorsy.

Although it seems like a lot, this security level is crucial when working with expensive vehicles like motorhomes.

Organizations like this will provide this and a lot of other services, and this makes RV sharing between renters and owners a safe and stress-free process.

CHAPTER 3-
HOW TO TAKE THE LEAP AND TRANSITION INTO THE RV LIFESTYLE

With the right tools, transitioning into the RV lifestyle can be easy. Taking the wrong steps during this phase may end up leaving you frustrated, stranded, or even worse, in trouble with the law.

Let's now move forward and take a look at all of the crucial things to do before leaping.

RV GPS

GPS technology ensures smooth and easy traveling. However, RV owners still have concerns about using these devices, because, in comparison to your average vehicles, RVs are heavier, taller and longer, and a GPS that is meant for vehicles can lead the RV owner into serious issues.

Towing or driving an RV can be a horrible experience when the GPS directs you to a bridge not suited for your RVs weight, a low overpass, or residential areas with low tree branches.

However, before choosing a GPS device for your RV, there are a few things you need to consider. Let's take a look at what they are below.

Types of RV GPS

There is a range of GPS systems that you can use in your RV:

- **Street Navigation System**

    This kind of GPS ensures that you do not get lost immediately as you begin driving your RV. This device offers turn by turn instructions, including your mileage, speed, and estimated arrival time.

- **Handheld GPS Systems**

    This is a great option if you want a more convenient approach when traveling on the road. Having this in handy can have a huge impact on your outdoor travels. Regardless of how unfamiliar a specific location is, it minimizes the possibility of getting lost. It can also offer you accurate position information that you can easily send to rescuers in case of an emergency.

- **Sports GPS System**

    If you are a sports fan aside from a full-time RVer, then this is a great choice. It can also be useful to you in marine environments.

Choosing a GPS

Consider the following things when you choose the best GPS for your needs.

- **Size**

    A portable GPS is great for your RV as you can transport it with ease. Some models come in the size of wallets. The screen should be of the appropriate size in order to let you drive without hassle while still being able to see the info displayed. If you spend a lot of time on the road, a 4-inch diagonal screen is ideal.

- **Controls**

    It is important to check out the controls of the GPS device before choosing one. Also, find out if you can easily operate the controls.

- **Installation process**

    Check how easy it is to install the device. Also, look into mounting options. These are crucial when making a choice.

- **Wi-Fi and Bluetooth**

    Although those are optional, having these features is crucial in enhancing a unit's reliability. It is also a convenient option as it easily lets you pair up the device with your tablet or smartphone.

- **Predictive data entry**

    This feature allows you to do your searches quickly and with ease. It also gives you the addresses you search for the most frequently just by putting in the first letters. This feature adds an extra benefit as it helps to enhance safety while on the road.

Getting Internet Access on Your RV

Having access to the internet in the RV is becoming more crucial, as most RVers want to be able to send emails and stay online. There are many choices when it comes to internet connectivity:

Dial-Up, Cable RV DSL, Internet Access

Previously, plugging to a dial-up modem at a campground was one of the only ways to get internet access on an RV. But now, although still an option, it does not meet the requirements of most RVers, as it has many limitations and slow speed.

Another method is to utilize the internet access you can find in public locations, which is a great choice if you are not a full-time RVer. It can also be a back-up plan if you have no alternative.

Campgrounds sometimes provide cable or phone connections for RV internet access at their various sites. Normally, the visiting RVer will need to call the cable or phone company to activate these connections. If you are planning to stay on the campground for a while, this can be a great option. If you are passing through, it is not a great option to stay connected on the road.

WiFi RV Internet Access

This is a major improvement in RV internet access. Many laptops come with built-in 802.11 capacity, a Wi-Fi adapter, or a card, and these should be able to provide you with internet access right from your RV.

Many parks offer wireless hotspots where you can get internet access. You can also find this in many restaurants, convenience stores, among other places. Some require a password while others are public.

Cellular RV Internet Access

Another option is to utilize a cell phone provider for internet access. Providers consist of companies like Sprint, Verizon, T-Mobile, and AT&T among others.

In its easiest form, you can use a phone with data capability to browse the web and retrieve emails. You get internet access via the wireless provider, using one of the numerous monthly plans that they offer.

Also, you can use your cell phone as a modem to get internet access in your RV. Here, you connect the cell phone to your computer via Bluetooth or USB cable. This means of connection provides you with a larger screen. You can also utilize a wireless router to offer access to numerous PCs.

Finally, you can use a wireless networking device. Most wireless providers offer devices and plans that let you connect, with options for how much data you want.

Remember that numerous wireless providers often offer separate data and voice coverage maps. Ensure you check out their websites for more details.

Satellite RV Internet Access

Using a satellite system which you mount on the rooftop or as a distinct auxiliary unit is another way of getting access to the internet. Wherever you are, you will have access to the internet. However, these are expensive options.

There four core providers of satellite internet are the following:

- Starband
- HughesNet/Direcway
- Skyway
- Wildblue

Most RVers usually go with HughesNet as their satellite provider.

Getting Cell Phone Coverage on Your RV

Cell phone providers

As a full-time RVer, there are four core providers for cell phone service you can choose from. The main difference between each of these carriers is how widespread their coverage is around the country.

These providers include;

- **Verizon**

    It offers the most 4G coverage in the country, so it is usually a great choice for travelers. It has the most organized LTE and typically great overall performance.

If you are going to select a network, the benefits it offers makes it the top choice.

- **AT&T**

    It is the next largest carrier and works great in complementing Verizon if you like being on the road. However, its LTE is not as fast as Verizon, but there are numerous areas in the country where it performs perfectly. Sometimes, it is the only choice you have.

    While on the road, combining AT&T and Verizon will provide you with the broadest coverage.

- **T-Mobile**

    T-Mobile is a rapidly growing network. The major drawback with this carrier is the absence of raw coverage, especially indoors and in rural areas. In areas where there is coverage, its network speeds are consistently fast.

- **Sprint**

    Sprint is another great carrier, but its coverage is only useful when closer to larger cities. However, roaming agreements with T-mobile may change this.

Regional Carriers

Aside from the four large national carriers, there is a range of smaller local and regional carriers that own and run their networks.

Some of the bigger ones include:

- Cellular One
- Cellcom
- C-Spire Wireless
- U.S. Cellular
- nTelos

These regional carriers are not usually a great option for travelers. However, there are certain locations where they have a great presence. Even if the regional carrier offers coverage around the country via roaming agreements, if you are using the service outside of its core region, you will deal with all kinds of limitations and restrictions.

RV Driver License Requirements

Some people may tell you that you only require a regular license to travel in an RV. For most cases, this is true, but not always. There are many different things that contribute to the kind of license you require. These could range from:

- The weight of the vehicle

- The state(s) you plan on traveling to
- The weight of your RV
- The length of your RV

RVs that weigh less than 26,000 pounds don't require a unique license in any of the 50 states. However, if the weight of your RV is beyond that, you may require a special license.

So, even though in numerous situations you won't have to bother about meeting any license needs, there are situations that would require it. Aside from the factors that determine when and where you will require a special license, you also need to consider two classes of licenses: non-commercial and commercial.

Which States Need a Special License?

The states below need a unique license if you plan on driving an RV. However, you should note that every one of these states does not have similar requirements. Some need different classes of licenses and have diverse requirements in regards to weight and length.

It is always a great idea to check out the specific laws of your state before hitting the road. The states that need a different license are the following:

- California
- Wyoming

- Washington, D.C.
- Pennsylvania
- Nevada
- Michigan
- New Mexico
- Maryland
- North Carolina
- Texas

Do You Require a CDL to Drive an RV?

CDLs or commercial driver licenses are unique kinds of licenses needed to drive commercial vehicles like city buses. However, you also require a CLD to drive an RV. A few states require a commercial license for RVs which clock in at more than the peak weight requirements.

They are:

- Indiana
- Connecticut
- Kansas
- South Carolina
- Wisconsin
- Michigan

- Hawaii
- New-York

Note that the precise requirements in every state may differ and you should check it out before heading there. Another thing you may need to determine is if you require a CDL to drive an RV that runs on air brakes. However, air brakes do not determine whether you require an exclusive license even though some states may need you to attain an air brake endorsement on your license.

Do You Require a Special License to Drive a Class C RV?

To avoid dealing with the hassles that come with these complex licensing laws, you can go with an RV that is less than 26,000 pounds, as this ensures that you won't require a different license.

Also, almost every class C RV falls under the weight requirement for a standard driver license, and it is highly unlikely to find one that needs an exclusive license. They are also great to drive and are the ideal choice for starters.

How To Get Your Mail While On The Road

This is something you will need to figure out, especially if you will have to pay bills while on the road.

Why you should create your domicile

In the US, a permanent address is required for all activities. RV parks will also request this information, and this can be tedious when you live in your RV full-time. You need to have a permanent address for voting, taxes, insurance, etc. which is why you will have to set up a domicile before heading out.

Domicile is a country that an individual categorizes as their permanent home or resides in and has a reasonable connection with. Your domicile is your new address. Three crucial states are great domiciles; Florida, Texas and South Dakota.

Choosing your domicile state

If you're from these RV-friendly states, you are in luck. However, the state you select is completely dependent on you. Because laws differ between states, below are some crucial factors to put into consideration when selecting your state:

- Taxes like vehicle, sales, and income tax
- Registration and vehicle inspection laws
- Jury Duty
- Renewals of driver's license
- Homeschooling laws if you have children on the road
- The location you plan to travel to

Where you plan to travel to is crucial if the state you select requires yearly visits to update your vehicle inspection. This may be stressful depending on the new state you plan on heading to.

Establishing your domicile

There are numerous services that can help you establish your domicile. A great option is Escapes, and they can set it up on your behalf in any of the states we have just mentioned above. They also do more than just forwarding your emails.

My Dakota Address is a great pick if you are in South Dakota and for Florida, St Brendan's Isle is a great choice.

Escapees will offer you a permanent mailing address. They will even ensure that your mail gets forwarded to you on the road. Once you find a convenient service, it becomes quite easy to get your emails on the road.

Once you set up your address, you will go through the process of switching the address on all your official documents such as your bills, driver's license, insurance, etc.

Getting your mail while roaming

Ok, you now have an address to collect your mail, so a practical step would be to reduce the amount of mail you get before you begin traveling.

Convert statements and bills to electronic and ensure you will be able to make payments online. Get yourself off mailing lists and stop all subscriptions. Urge your friends and family to utilize emails instead of snail mail.

Irrespective of the situation, mail will require additional time get to you as it's getting forwarded from another address. Ensure you know when specific bills are due, like insurance policy renewals.

To get mail while on the road, below are your options:

- **Local Family and Friends**

    If you will be paying a visit to a place where you know someone, request if you can utilize their address. If they agree, inform your mail forwarding service of the address. Also, ensure you give them lots of time for the mail to get to you before heading to your next location.

- **Current Location**

    The majority of the locations you are paying to reside in will allow you to use their address to get your mail, whether it's a hostel, campground or hotel. For this purpose, some campgrounds offer you a real mailbox. Just ensure your unit number and name is indicated in the shipping address.

- **Rent PO Boxes**

If you have plans to remain in one location for a long period, it may be easy for you to rent a PO Box or a personal mailbox at the local post office. This is not expensive, and all you will have to do is use that address for everything you want to receive.

Note that you will have to change the address if you move.

- **Commercial Receivers**

Some organizations, like UPS Stress and FedEx Office can also get packages on your behalf. This is the case if you are their client. Call and make inquiries at the office you plan on receiving your mail at in regards to their policies and procedures.

- **US Postal Service**

Whether you plan on being on the road in your RV for a weekend or full-time, the U.S Postal service provides a range of different options.

If you want to stay in a specific location for a while, you will be able to install a mailbox for your mail to be delivered straight to your RV.

If you prefer not to rent a post office box or change your address, you have the option of putting your mail on hold. Your local post office is able to hold your mail for as long as 30 days.

RVing offers great freedom, but you cannot ignore all the responsibilities in your life. With mailing options available to choose from, you can take your RV anywhere while still taking care of your personal and financial obligations.

Getting packages while on the road

If you plan on getting packages on the road, there are many great options.

If you are RVing, Amazon Prime can be your friend, as it is the easiest way to get any package on the road.

Netflix disc shipment service is also a friendly option for RVers. As long as you don't forget to change your address when they get your last return disc, they will be able to ship it to your next address. Also, they have distribution centers all around the US. It is a great method to watch new movies and TV series while on the road.

RV Insurance – What Kind of Insurance Do You Need For Your RV?

The most puzzling aspect of RV ownership is trying to decide if the standard auto insurance will provide you with adequate coverage and if you require RV insurance.

But the truth is, there are a host of easy options to select from and depending on the kind of RV you own, you may not need insurance.

After all, RV insurance is not similar to a car or home insurance.

The major difference in coverage needs is straightforward. If you can tow it, insurance is likely not mandatory. And if you can get it from one location to another without the assistance of another vehicle, you will most likely need to buy insurance coverage.

Ultimately, any vehicle driven on the road needs insurance and motorhomes are included. You will need to have minimum liability for your state to drive on the road legally. More coverage is optional and available except if a lender requires it.

The following is RV coverage you can choose from:

- Standard Motor Home Coverage
- Collision
- Limited Property Damage
- Uninsured Motorist
- Property Damage Liability and Bodily Injury
- Property Protection

- Comprehensive
- Personal Injury Protection (PIP)

Since you don't drive campers on their own and tow them behind a vehicle, it is not compulsory to get RV insurance according to a majority of the states' laws. Only a lender may want full coverage to safeguard its interest, so if you used a loan to purchase your RV, you can be sure that it is necessary to have full coverage.

For a newer camper, carrying full coverage is ideal in order not to lose your investment. But, if you have no secured loan, the coverage is not compulsory.

Standard Coverage for Campers

Coverage against physical damage for a camper is similar to a car. Options include:

- Comprehensive
- Collision

Specialized Coverage

Specialized coverage can be useful at the period of loss. For example loss of personal effects. Things you may not consider before a claim like personal effects and custom equipment can be pricey if there is no coverage in your RV policy.

Lots of organizations provide specialized coverage on both campers and motorhomes.

Options include:

- Total Loss Replacement
- Vacation Liability
- Roadside Assistance
- Custom Equipment
- Personal Effects

Total loss replacement

This is available only to RVs which are previously untitled up to a model-year-old which means RVs which are just a year older than their model year or year of production.

Other RVs are insured for actual cash value or agreed value. A claim may be tedious enough so ensure you understand your insurance policy so you are aware when a loss occurs.

Custom equipment

Custom equipment is essential for RVs that have custom parts. If you've made upgrades to your RV, you may want to elevate the automatic limit. A standard policy usually has a coverage limit of $1000. Custom equipment is not cheap and can go past the standard limit with ease. If you customize your RV, monitor the amount and invest in custom parts.

Vacation liability

It is usually added alongside a $10,000 set limit, as long as you select collision and comprehensive coverage. It pays up to limits specified for damage to property and bodily injury due to an accident that occurs while the RV is functioning as a temporary vacation residence.

Roadside assistance

Roadside assistance provides coverage for towing a damaged RV. It offers to tow to the closest qualified facility at the location and time of disablement when RVs get damaged as a result of:

- Mechanical or electrical breakdown
- Lock-out
- Flat tire
- Battery failure
- Insufficient supply of, water, fuel oil or other fluids
- Entrapment in water, sand, snow, or mud, water within 100 feet of the roadway

Personal effects

This will provide coverage for your belongings in case of a loss while taking a vacation in an RV. A homeowner's policy may provide coverage for your belongings, but deductibles are applicable.

How much RV Insurance do you require?

You need to consider the following when deciding how much insurance you require:

- The things you need to protect
- If you own custom features
- Where you plan to travel
- If you are using the RV full time or part-time

The best answer is that you are going to require as much as you can afford to offer protection for yourself, your RV, guests, and personal property.

It is ideal to evaluate your requirements and decide on a number or talk to a licensed agent to get an accurate quote for insurance.

Other forms of Insurance for the RV Owner & his Family

It can be very entertaining to be on the road for long periods of time. However, it is crucial to remember that traditional insurance is still crucial. Some of these include:

Life Insurance

Life insurance is absolutely crucial because you will be on the road a lot and will be traveling to unknown locations. Therefore, your risk is always going to be higher than someone who stays at home.

Disability Insurance

Getting disability insurance is crucial, because you never know when an accident or sickness that might hamper your ability to work and make income may occur.

Health Insurance & Dental Coverage

Your health insurance provides coverage if you are hurt or ill in an accident. It can also help you cover any gaps that could occur if you only had the medical coverage via your RV insurance.

You also need to note your dental health while on the road and be certain to get a great dental plan because dental health is crucial irrespective of where you are.

CHAPTER 4- PREPPING TIPS TO GET STARTED FULL TIME

In the previous chapter, you learned how to get ready when transitioning into the RV lifestyle. In this chapter, we will be learning various tips to help you get started on your trip full-time.

RV Tanks- What Kind of Tanks Do You Need for Your RV?

RVing can lead you to some amazing locations and create great memories. However, not every aspect of RVing is appealing. Emptying and maintaining your septic tank regularly is not fun, but it's crucial. Think of it as part of the RV adventure.

If you do not take care of this system properly, things can quickly go south.

Regardless of whether you plan on renting an RV or if you are a new RV owner, it is crucial to learn how to care for your RV tanks properly. Below are a few things that can help you begin.

What does the septic system of an RV look like?

Recreational vehicles come with three tanks which can be found underneath the RV to ensure things go smoothly.

They are freshwater, black and grey tanks:

- Freshwater tank

    This is a tank to store fresh water. It is the water that comes out of the RV taps for cooking and bathing.

- Grey Water Tank

    The tank helps in holding the dirty water from your RV kitchen sink and shower. Some used vintage RVs and campers do not come with this tank.

- Black Water Tank

    New RVers often find the Black Water Tank scary. This tanks aid in holding wastewater coming from the toilet. If your RV does not come with a grey tank, all kinds of dirty water get into this.

If not properly maintained, any of these tanks can cause issues.

How frequently should you empty your tanks?

This is relative. If you are traveling in a large group, this is something you may have to do frequently. If it is only you and your spouse, once a week is enough.

A general rule is to hold on till your tanks are two-thirds full before you begin to empty them. It brings about a more seamless flow when you dump and ensures the process is more effective.

Newer RVs come with systems that let you know precisely how filled your tanks are. It is an ideal method to gauge when to dump but note that after a while, the sensors may not always function properly. Even new ones may provide inaccurate readings because of waste and paper sticking to the sensor which makes it say it is full even when it isn't. It is crucial to observe the amount of waste you are collecting.

Emptying your RV tanks

The holding tanks should be very visible on your RV. If you are renting one, ensure you ask the RV owner for information.

Before your initial waste water dump, ensure you have a sewer hose and gloves to keep your hands secure.

Next, be certain to point out the valves on the outer part of your RV. They will be clearly marked with 'grey' and 'black.'

Connect your sewer hose to the RV valve. Take the other part and connect it to the sewer you are utilizing. Before you pull the valves, ensure it is tightened at both ends.

Begin with the black tank. Note that the wastewater from your toilet goes straight to this tank. Ensure you do not dump the water from this tank in any location other than designated dump stations. These are hard to miss because they come with clear markings.

To empty it, pull the valve and allow the tank to drain. When you can't hear liquid dripping from the hose anymore, close the valve. Make sure you completely close the valve as leaving it open is a bad idea, because it will result in liquids flowing out, and there would be no means of draining out the solids.

Next, do same with the gray tank. Some individuals leave the gray valve tank open and allow it to drain constantly. This is not ideal because when you flush the gray tank first, it aids in flushing any solids trapped in your sewer hose. If you do not close this valve, you won't have the additional water to clean out the sewer hose after dumping the black tank.

To ensure clean-up is easy, go slowly when loosening the sewer hose. Lots of RVers use a tub or bucket to contain the hose when idle.

Maintaining the septic system in your RV

You will be able to find starter kits at RV stores or at Walmart. Once you understand how to empty the tanks on your RV, the process will be much easier. However, there is more to tank maintenance than simply emptying them. Maintenance is crucial as it will prevent to have issues in the future.

Generally, frequently flushing alongside sanitizing and cleaning your tanks will ensure that your system runs efficiently.

Other things to Note about your RV tanks:

Fresh Water Tank

This is not as scary as the other three tanks, but it still requires frequent maintenance. When you fill the tank, ensure only to use a portable water hose. They can easily be spotted because their color is white. With this tank, it is crucial to observe the weather. Insulate your hose when the weather is freezing and drain your fresh water when it is extremely hot to avert water stagnation.

Cleaning the fresh water tank

If the tank starts to smell, there might be contamination. Clean the tank with household bleach; pour in a quarter cup of bleach for every 15 gallons of water still in the tank. Keep running until you get rid of all the bleached water, then let the tank sit for a day. Fill in your tank with water and let it run until the smell of bleach vanishes, then use as normal.

Gray Water Tank

In huge fifth wheels and travel trailers, there may be more than one gray tank. It is crucial to note that it comes with a very small drain. Ensure particles of food do not go down the drain. Even particles as little as peas may lead to a blockage.

Black Water Tank

The following are a few tips to reduce the issues you have with this black tank:

- Utilize only single-ply toilet paper. Two-ply can lead to blockage in the tank.
- Flush frequently. Ensure you always add water to the toilet bowl before you flush.
- After dumping, sanitize your tank. You can search for chemicals that do this in the RV section of any major store.

- Ensure you clean this tank frequently by placing a garden hose into the toilet. It should aid in flushing your system and clearing up build-ups.

RV Jacks – Why Do You Need One?

If you have ever gotten to the RV campground or park and noticed that your site is not even, you will know how crucial parking on level ground is. RVs come with in-built features that you can use to deal with uneven parking plots or spots, like RV Jacks or stabilizers.

If you are new to the world of RVing, let us take a look at how they work and when to utilize them.

RV Jacks – What are they?

These are a bunch of jacks that aid in preventing the vertical and lateral movement of your RV. They are mostly utilized in towable RVs like fifth wheels and travel trailers.

These stabilizers are frequently constructed into the chassis beneath the body of your RV. You will also be able to activate them from the internal part of the RV. These RV jacks can come in manual or motorized form. There are numerous kinds of RV jacks, ranging from the slide out, to scissor jacks, and universal jacks.

The kind of jacks you will require depend on the kind of RV you are using. When purchasing an RV, if the one you like does not come with stabilizers, you may purchase one. They're a little pricey but are definitely worth it.

Ensure you purchase the appropriate RV jacks for your trailer type or motorhome. It may look like an extra cost that you can ignore, but when you park on an uneven surface, it may damage your RV.

How to use RV stabilizers

These tools are often used with wheel chocks alongside a range of devices for leveling to ensure the RV is as level and stable as possible. With stabilizing jacks, the rocking motion you normally feel would be a thing of the past when you walk around your RV. You won't have to bother about items moving around each time you dive on the RV bed.

While chocks and other systems can ensure your RV is level, using stabilizers is the best method because of the location that they are set up beneath your RV.

The type of stabilizer you use will depend on the RV you use. Some stabilizers are universal, but it is advised to first carry out your research to locate the stabilizer that it most suitable for your RV. Dependent on the width, length and amount of slide outs, as well as your tires, you may require precise kinds of RV jacks to be certain that you remain level no matter where you head.

You can go on RV forums or contact your manufacturers to know what kind of stabilizers are best suited for your RV. You can also get recommended stabilizing options from your RV dealer when you head to the lot.

When to use RV stabilizers

You can use RV stabilizers any time you park on an uneven surface, including grass, dirt, and gravel. Depending on the location where you park your RV, you will notice that even asphalt pads and concrete are not even as a result of deterioration.

In these situations, stabilizers are also great. The moment you park your rig, you can immediately move around in the RV to instantly let you know when you need to use your stabilizers.

Stabilizers would also be required for some kinds of RVs. Towable vehicles, like travel trailers, fifth wheels and campers will only have minimal contact with the ground you are parking on. Stabilization can aid in preventing shifting when you park. Fifth wheels are the ideal candidates for stabilizers. This is because of the weight placement on the body of the fifth wheel. However, many other trailers can also use them.

The lighter your RV is, the more likely it requires stabilizers. A trailer or a heavy RV will utilize its weight to stabilize itself on the ground, while RVs with less weight don't have that benefit. This means they have a higher likelihood of moving about if you move inside. Other kinds of lighter coaches also need stabilizers.

Having a stable RV is crucial if you own an absorption refrigerator. These kinds of fridges need to stay level, or you may end up causing damage you can't fix, and no one wants to spend money on new gadgets. Ensure you know what kind of refrigerator is in your RV before you purchase it. This will allow you to know the measure to take when leveling and parking.

RV Packing Tips for Newbies

If you are heading on an RV camping trip for the first time, or just starting full-time RVing, you are likely feeling excited. However, you are likely to also feel a little overwhelmed. From learning the intricacies of using an RV to pulling a trailer or motorhome for the first time, there are many things you need to keep in mind when planning for a trip on your RV for the first time.

The following are a few tips that can help:

Make a checklist

One of the things many individuals finds stressful is packing. Newbies are worried that they may not pack everything they will require. At the same time, others are worried about overpacking and going beyond the weight limits of the RV.

The great news is that packing an RV does not have to be as tedious as people make it seem. Below are a few tips that can help with packing:

Play out your day mentally

Start the process of packing by playing out your daily activities mentally. Consider what you will require and start to make a list. Items many people tend to forget including folding chairs, bedding, RV toilet paper, and cookware.

Also keep in mind that this is not a huge home, so you may be unable to pack all the things you require.

Add Entertainment

This is another thing lots of individuals tend to ignore. While singing, hiking and exploring is likely to take up most of your time, you will still need some downtime, especially if you are going to be living here full-time.

For this reason, things like books, board games, smartphones, etc. are great to have in handy.

Grab Some Snacks

It's not always easy to find reasonably priced groceries in little towns where you tend to find campgrounds. So, it is always a great idea to stock up your fridge or pantry before heading there.

Also, it is essential to run your refrigerator for a couple of days before planning to stock up to be certain that it's cold. Storing a bottle of water in the fridge during those days will aid with the cooling process.

Pack Evenly

Even though most individuals are scared of surpassing the weight limits of the RV, a more common issue is loading unevenly. A motorhome or trailer that is not evenly loaded has a higher possibility of experiencing a tire blowout.

To prevent this problem, be certain to place a heavy material on one part of the RV with an item that has similar weight on the opposite part of the RV.

Hopefully, these tips can help you get started full time and go in completely relaxed and prepared. This is the proper way of beginning to live in an RV full-time.

Things to do before leaving

- Place contact information for emergencies in the wallet of each traveler
- Credit card, traveler's cheque, and cash
- Cell phone with additional battery/charger

- Your RV Checklist
- General equipment for camping
- Maps, GPS and Compass
- First Aid Kit and Prescription Medicine
- Camera and Accessories
- Weather radio
- Whistle for each individual in case of emergencies
- Alarm clock and battery
- Flashlights and extra batteries
- Folding Knife
- Firewood and tools to cut it
- Sunscreen and Sunglasses
- Backpack/daypack
- Binoculars
- Bug spray
- Sleeping bags
- Lantern
- Candles
- Bedding which includes sheets, pillows, and blankets
- Basic work tools

Clothing Items

- Undergarments
- Hats, gloves, and caps
- Shoes/socks
- Warm and cold weather clothes
- Boots for hiking and thick socks
- Sleepwear/slippers
- Rain gear

Items for Hygiene

- Shaving kit
- Toothbrush / toothpaste
- Toilet paper
- Deodorant
- Shampoo and Soap
- Towel
- Laundry bag
- Mirror

Kitchen Items

- Comprehensive Meal Plan
- Groceries

- Utensils, cups, dishes
- Condiments
- Camping Stove
- Lighter fluid for charcoal
- Burner
- Aluminum foil
- Lighter
- Pots, pans, skillets
- Can opener
- Grill and fuel (propane, charcoal)
- Dishwashing items
- Airtight containers (to keep animals away)
- Ice chest and ice
- Trash bags
- Ziploc bags

Checklist for Your Pets

- Pet food
- Pet toys
- Leash and harness
- Treats

- Blanket and bed
- Water and food bowl
- Water
- Plastic bags to pick up after the dog
- Towel

Meeting Your Power Requirements on The Road

If you plan on residing in an RV that is connected to the grid, you are in luck, as you will have unlimited electricity. However, if this is not the case, you need to come up with some kind of power solution.

RV Electrical Systems

Most RVs come with two electrical systems. There is the DC or direct control system which works similar to your car, and there is the AC or alternating system which is similar to the one in your home.

The AC system runs when you connect your trailer to an outside AC power source, while the DC system functions using one or more of the battery systems fitted into your RV. Your fans, water pump, TV, and fans work using the DC power system. Large appliances like microwaves, air conditioners, and power outlets get power from the AC power system.

The AC system can generate a higher level of power than the DC system which is restricted by your RV batteries. The two systems are set up in a way that if there is AC power getting into your RV, it will also charge the batteries for the DC system. The device responsible for doing this is known as a converter. Many RVs come with an inverter which is a device that transforms DC power into AC. RVs that have inverters will come with wall outlets that are specially marked and run on the DC battery system but offer AC power.

The majority of RVs are constructed in a way that if you have shore power, you will be able to run anything in the RV. The DC system will be able to run necessities like the water pump and light for a couple days, as long as you manage it properly.

Power Sources for Your RV

The following are a few ways to meet your RV power requirements:

Purchase a quality generator

When plugged into your AC system, generators function similarly to Shore Power, and they offer AC power. They don't usually offer the amount of power you get from shore power, but it depends on the size of the generator.

Generators come in watts rather than amps. A generator of 1000w is great for a little RV or if you don't plan on running heavy systems like an air conditioner. A generator of 3,500w can run the majority of systems on many RVs. You also have the capacity to daisy chain a few 1000w generators to get more power.

If you overdraw a generator, the risk is not the same as on shore power. Overdrawing a generator won't offer you adequate power to run everything the right way, and you could even ruin some of your appliances.

Some motorhomes come with built-in generators. These are different from the actual engine which runs your RV. These can be especially useful if they are insulated and not that noisy. Some parks often limit external generators because of the noise. This is the case mostly at night. The most important thing to keep in mind when using external generators is to never use them indoors. They create lots of carbon monoxide gas, and it can quickly become dangerous in an enclosed space, so it is advised to always run them outside.

Having a power generator offers you the freedom to do as much work as you like. Go for a generator that is not too bulky so can move around with ease. Check out reviews for the leading portable generator reviews.

Let's take a quick look at each of the power sources of an RV.

Your RV Batteries

Every RV will come with a set of batteries. These offer your RV a source of power when there is no external power. The amount of power the batteries will be able to offer by themselves is quite minimal. They can run the water pump, lights and little appliances for most of the day, but that's it. You will be unable to run the heating systems or air conditioner. It will also quickly drain when using heavy appliances like the microwave.

Your battery charges every time you connect an external power source to your RV. This consists of vehicle engines, shore power, solar power, and generators. When you are on the move, your vehicle engine will help charge your batteries.

Shore Power

Shore power is when you can connect your RV into an AC electrical grid. The available power you have the capacity of drawing is measured in Amps. RV connections are usually 20amps and 50amps. You will be able to connect your RV to an electric line from the home of someone else. However, be careful as home outlets are usually just 15 amps.

Your RV will be able to utilize 30amps or 50amps. Larger RVs are typically set up to utilize 50amps. You will be able to use your RV with a lower Amp source, but it is dangerous if you are not careful. If you are using a source which is lower than what your RV was created for, you may wreck the electrical system if you try to draw in more power than what the line on the shore power is rated for. You could blow your fuses and even wreck your RV's power source.

When you use the shore power you find at an RV park, there should be a circuit breaker close by. Ensure that you turn it off when you connect and off when you disconnect.

Solar and wind

The crucial thing to note about sources of renewable energy is that they are developed to charge your batteries rather than offer you on-demand power. They aid in generating DC current as opposed to the AC you attain from generators and shore power.

For this reason, you will still be limited by the level of power your battery can offer, but you will be able to keep it going for a more extended period because you can recharge as you use. This offers you an off the grid source of power, and it's especially great and cost effective if you are RVing full-time.

The benefit is that you are continually charging your batteries. However, the drawback is that you won't be able to run anything more power demanding, which you would be able to do if you were just running the battery system on its own. This rules out the microwave, air conditioner, and other heavy hitters.

RV Driving Tips

New RV drivers always find out very quickly that driving an RV is very different from driving a car.

Navigation of parking spaces, bridges, right turns and gas stations in your RV will require patience, practice, and even some courage.

Below are a few RV driving tips you should note:

How to Turn

Your RV is wide and long. This means your turns will have to be broad and long as well. This is the case especially for right turns because you will be dealing with curbs.

Always keep an eye on your rear-view mirrors and stay as close to the center lane as possible. Do not rush this, being slow is okay. Don't bother with the traffic you are creating; it's better to do it slowly and right than to deal with damages you will be facing for a long time.

How to Brake

Always note that when braking your huge RV, it won't be as fast as braking your car. Therefore, you will have to maintain more distance from the vehicles ahead of you, and you should carefully watch out for possible issues so you can instantly react to whatever you may be facing.

On downgrades, ensure you downshift and allow your engine to help do as much of the braking as possible when trying to stop. The enhanced engine resistance in a lower gear will help you slow your vehicle down while minimizing your brake's wear and tear.

How to Park

If you are unable to see properly, stop. Ask someone to help direct you to a parking spot. There is nothing wrong with using a spotter, and even the most experienced RVers do it when they have to.

Take all the time you need, and use your spotter or mirrors properly. If you can, stay away from restricted spots. Move to an easier parking spot even if this means you will have to park a little further.

If you are towing, note that when you back up, the trailer turns to the opposite end of your steering wheel.

How To Determine Your Lane Position

Are you moving too far to the right or left in your lane? Your RV is quite wide, so it can be difficult to determine the proximity of the passenger side to the shoulder. It can be quite puzzling in the beginning, but with time, you will begin to know the width and the lane position will just come naturally.

Till then, observe your mirrors and note how close your rear tires are to the lane markers. Whenever you can, remain in the right lane, move slowly, and concentrate on the traffic close to you on the left.

Going Through Bridges

You'd be amazed at how frequently RVers fail to watch out for the bridge clearance. Know the height of your vehicle and watch out for low bridges. Plan the routes you wish to take using a GPS device for your RV that lets you know where low bridges are and plan routes to keep you away from them.

Going Through High Grades & Mountains

In mountains, reduce your speed. Use low gears especially when heading downhill and uphill. Remain in the right lane and don't bother with other cars going past you.

When heading downhill, be sure that your car does not start going too fast. Leave it in low gear and keep the speed of your RV down.

Using Gas Stations

You want to take your motorhome to truck stops and not just any kind of gas station. Lots of stations are not constructed to accommodate the width or height of your RV, and you may spend lots of time trying to get past the pumps.

Many new RV drivers have wrecked their sides, roofs and fenders making efforts to pull up to the pump.

The crucial part of learning RV driving is to go easy and utilize your mirrors. Do not worry about being slower than others. It's best to be safe and slow than quick and risky.

Once you do this, with time, driving your RV will start to become natural, and you will begin to enjoy every part of RVing.

Also, there are many fantastic training resources and schools for new RV drivers, so check them out to become a better RV driver.

CHAPTER 5 -
FINANCIAL PREPARATIONS

RVing is not that cheap. Regardless of whether you plan to live on a budget while RVing or not, you still need to meet a few important financial obligations.

Below are a few financial arrangements you need to put in place to ensure your life on the road is successful.

Important Financial Preparations

The RV choices, as well as your lifestyle, will have a very strong influence on whatever the answer to this question will be. It is a very personal thing.

However, we will be focusing on typical budget line items. Also, I will be placing an estimated average budget expense for every month.

Monthly Budgets and Less Frequent Expenses

You can develop a 30-day budget. Although a lot of expenses don't occur on a monthly basis, you can simplify them into monthly expenses for the sake of your budget, and to ensure that that amount is a part of your savings on a monthly basis.

By doing so, you will make sure that you do not have any problem when facing expenses.

RV Gear/ Modifications

There is no guarantee that the RV dealership that you do business with will make provisions for the primary gear that you need to travel and live in an RV.

For convenience and safety, you may also need to ensure to make some specific upgrades. If you purchased a used RV, for example, you may need to make a few additional changes that will cost you some money.

A lot of RVers prefer off-grid camping and like to boondock. These are the types of people that love getting their RV outfitted with solar power. Others use painting and remodeling and also change fabrics and flooring to ensure it feels like theirs.

RV payment

RV repairs and maintenance – It does not matter if your RV has a guarantee, as saving some money on a monthly basis for things that are not included in the guarantee cannot be overemphasized.

Some of these things include generator maintenance, water filters, wiper blades, oil changes, etc. You should make all these expenses a part of your budget. This is kind of like upgrading homes made from sticks and bricks to make life more comfortable.

RV Insurance

It is advised to make your RV your full-time abode as this will ensure that insurance covers you not only for the RV but also for the contents of the RV. If it is financed, it is imperative that you get your RV insured for its full pay off value.

If it isn't, you have to come up with what you think its replacement value is. Like for car insurance, you have the freedom to go ahead and select your deductibles.

Fuel

If you own a motorhome, you should have a budget for fuel. There is no fixed budget for this. Your budget for fuel is hugely dependent on how often you make use of your motorhome, as well as how far you go with it.

Tolls

In the United States, toll roads are gradually becoming popular. In many vicinities like Orlando, it is almost impossible to move around freely without making use of toll roads. Therefore, it's essential to plan ahead of time to ensure that you come up with ways to reduce costs.

On the North East coast, for example, you can buy EZ passes for tolls in grocery stores. This phenomenon is not peculiar to the Northeast coast and also happens in SunPass in Florida.

Annual Registration Fees

This is hugely dependent on your legal state of residence. In certain states, the annual registration fee is fixed. However, in a lot of other states, it is a tax that is dependent on your RV's value.

Propane

Do you plan on getting propane appliances such as ovens, stovetops, heaters or refrigerators? You will need to have a budget for propane. Your budget for propane will be dependent on how often you make use of any of the above-mentioned devices.

Generator Fuel

To be RVing comfortably, you need a generator. For this reason, you have to determine how often you plan to turn it on. Once you know this, you can determine a budget for it.

Financial Preparations for a Towed Vehicle

This is either the vehicle that gets towed at the back of your motorized RV or the car that is used to tow your fifth wheel or travel trailer.

- **Vehicle Payment:** This is like for RV's
- **Vehicle maintenance and repair:** This is like for RV'S
- **Vehicle gear/ modifications:** You might need to get a towing package installed on your vehicle and ensure that it's modified in order for your vehicle to be easily towed. You will also have to buy the necessary equipment.

Vehicle Fuel

If you have a towable, it is vital that you estimate the quantity of fuel that you will need on days that you have to move. This is dependent on how frequently you move and how much distance you cover. For vehicles that tow and cars that are being towed, you have to estimate fuel.

Tolls- Do not forget to include tolls for local travel, as certain parts of the country appear to be difficult to access without toll roads.

Storage

It is important to have a unit for storage. You will need to store items, including some that you will utilize in the future. With this in mind, it should be included in your monthly budget.

Campgrounds

The amount spent on campsites can be one of your most substantial regular expenses. It is, however, very dependent on your RVing pattern. Some of the general classes are contained below. Nevertheless, each of these categories has variables.

Resort Campgrounds

RV campgrounds that are styled like resorts come fully hooked up. This means they come with power, sewer, and water. Also, they often come with mini golfs, swimming pools, and other fun activities. Their cost is dependent on season, location, and amenities. Their prize can be as low as $30 and as high as $100 a night.

National and State Parks

National and state parks are usually located in amazing natural sites. Some national and state parks have a place for bathing, water, and power. Some even come with recreational centers with a bunch of different activities, large sites, and full hook-ups.

These national and state parks also have different costs. However, they are usually cheaper than resort campgrounds. Sometimes, it can be difficult to make reservations because of the enormous demand for them. An example of this is Florida state parks which give you the freedom to make reservations up to 11 months in advance. The price for a night at a national or state park ranges from $15 dollars to $48.

Boondocking

Boondocking means camping in the absence of hook-ups. This usually takes place in dispersed locations and is sometimes free or costs less than 15 dollars a night. There are actually many places to camp at for free in a tent or RV in the United States.

Some RV boondocking sites are national forests and Bureau of Land Management (BLM) land. Also, in the West, there are many free boondocking sites. However, in states that are located east of the Mississippi, they are very few.

Financial Plan for Food

The budget for food does not change for most people that are involved in RV full time. If you fall into the category of people that enjoy eating out, you are likely no to lose that habit as you travel. This group is broken into two various budget line materials for food-related expenses that take place monthly.

Groceries

There could be a difference in this figure because of factors such as location. The reason for this is because the costs change in different areas. Also, there could be variances in taxes. It is important to note that items that you can use in the house such as dishwashers, shampoos, and cleaners can all be considered separate line items. So, since they are purchased alongside groceries, they are included here as well.

Eating Out

Many people like to have a feel of the eateries in the locality as they travel. This is one aspect of traveling that you can always control. One fantastic thing about moving around in an RV is that you have the freedom to prepare the meals you eat, as they are equipped with refrigerating and cooking devices.

Insurance

RVer insurance exchange has a wealth of information for all full-time insurance needs that include RV/ autos and healthcare plans.

Health

The cost of insurance differs by state, the contribution of employers, and family size. As a result of this, there is a broad disparity in insurance costs. Therefore, you should carefully do an adequate study if you will be moving from one state to another on as you plan to go into the RV journey full time.

Life

Many people neglect life insurance due to the cost. In spite of this, if you have relatively good health, it is not expensive and can help your family if something unfortunate happens.

If an adult makes contributions to income, they should have the needed life insurance which can take care of the loss of a source of income, especially if there are unpaid debts such as car loans, credit cards, and mortgages. Also, every member of a family including children should have enough insurance to take care of expenses such as funerals which might be too expensive for families when they are grieving.

Mail Service

Although most things these days exist in electronic format, there are certain things that you can only send via mail. Many full-time RVers make use of the mail address of family members. Nevertheless, some others still make use of mailing services.

In reality, it does not matter which one you make use of. Whether this or the other, you will have to include this in your budget. This is because you need to reimburse family members if something has to be sent to you. For individuals that make use of mail services such as the ones escapees offer, your expense every month will be between $16.35 to $19.50. However, this is entirely dependent on the package that you are on.

Laundry

If your RV doesn't have a washer and a dryer, laundry has to be a part of your budget. To make a budget for laundry, find out how many loads you wash in a week. Once you get his number, multiply it by $3 to $5 for each load.

Clothing

You might think that you will not need to buy clothes. But you're wrong. As usual, you will be wearing your clothes every day, so they will wear out.

Although you obviously don't need to make this a part of your expense every month, it is essential that you put aside some money to replace worn out clothes.

Electronics

There are many electronic devices that you might want to include in your budget, such as subscriptions to streaming services like Netflix, satellite TV, cell phones, Internet devices, etc.

Cell Phone

There are many different cell phone plans, so ensure that you go through reviews and also look through coverage apps before choosing a plan, as this will help you determine the ideal carrier for you.

Internet Devices

Many RVers pay for hotspots and similar devices which come with monthly plans in order to have access to the internet. Although there are provisions for Wi-Fi in resort campgrounds, they cannot be relied on. If you need more information to help you make the right choice, you can count on the Mobile Internet Resource Centre.

Satellite Television

A lot of resort campgrounds have cable television. However, if you are working with a national and state park or a boondocking site, you might need satellite television to give you access to your favorite TV programs.

Streaming Subscriptions

There are many streaming services which will not stop charging you as you make the transition to RV life. As a result of this, always remember to include Netflix, Hulu, etc., in your budget if you want to make use of them.

Pets

All individuals that have pets are very much aware of the costs involved. These expenses are usually not cheap, so this should always be included in your budget.

Entertainment

Everyone loves fun. When on a journey to a new place, there is always the temptation to see absolutely everything and go everywhere you can. Therefore, it is vital to have a budget for entertainment.

Savings

When you think of the amount of money that you should save every month, always bear in mind that the more you save, the more you are in control of your destiny. Savings could include the following:

Emergency Funds

The aspect of savings that is considered most important is emergency funds. It is advised that you have savings for up to six months in a savings account. Although a lot of people do not agree with a savings account with an interest rate of 1%, this is much better than not having any savings or needing emergency credit which will have to be repaid at an interest rate of 10%.

Retirement

As soon as you are debt free and have a good amount aside as emergency funds, the next thing to consider is retirement savings. Based on Dave Ramsey's plan, you should put 15% of your gross income into tax-favored plans. Tax favored plans are those which let you keep your funds to a specific limit without having to pay tax. These include Roth IRAs and your firm's 401(k). You should not wait until you are about to retire to start saving for it.

Other Savings Goals

The following are other savings goals which can be made a part of your budget:

Christmas

This holiday appears to be the most expensive period of the year and this can badly affect your finances. To ensure that you are not negatively affected by Christmas, it is essential to save months ahead.

Special Occasions

Special occasions such as birthdays, Father's Day, etc. have to be planned for.

Vacations

RVers aren't excluded from vacations, as you can always save up some money for hotel reservations and airline tickets.

Monthly Financial Plan Sample

The table below is an example of what your financial plan should look like. Note that this is an estimate and it tends to differ between individuals.

Item	Monthly Average
Fund for RV and truck repair	$150
RV Insurance	$155

Truck Insurance	$100
Diesel Fuel	$150
Tolls	$40
Propane	$70
Campground fees	$300
Groceries	$150
Restaurants	$100
Health insurance	$150
Life Insurance	$75
Mail service	$8
Laundry	$25
Clothing	$15
Pets	$75
Entertainment	$150
Cell phone	$120
Satellite TV	$30
Streaming subscriptions	$11
Internet	$85

CHAPTER 6-
EARNING INCOME WHILE ON THE ROAD

Traveling in an RV is a remarkable experience. However, it can quickly become expensive, so it's a good idea to learn how to earn cash on the road.

This gives you the opportunity to fully enjoy your experience without having to bother about finances. In lots of cases, it implies that you will be able to live as comfortably as possible.

We will be taking a comprehensive look at all the methods to earn cash while you live in your RV full time. With the right planning and jobs, you will be able to live as comfortably as you can.

The idea is to locate what suits your skills and requirements. The great news is that there are so many options to choose from.

But before moving any further, you need to have a good plan. So, how do you do this? Keep reading to find out.

Do some planning and preparation

The very first step you need to take is to make a plan. Take time to reflect on ways to earn funds and what you will need to make this happen. You will also want to reflect on how this goes with your travel objectives.

Living in an RV often leaves you in the holiday spirit, and it can make it tedious to try to work simultaneously. Also, regardless of how you do it, making money takes time and dedication, so you will need to ensure you have the capacity and time to work.

One of the best methods is to create time solely for traveling or vacationing and dedicating other time for work. This is a little dependent on how you plan on earning, but it is an approach that works. Some of the methods we will be taking a look at will help sort out this issue for you.

Now that we have figured that out, let's take a look at ways that you can earn income.

Jobs on the move

There are many job opportunities all over the country if you know where to search. These will give you the opportunity to stop for a little, earn some cash, and continue with your trip.

Resorts and Summer Camps

These places will often offer travelers flexible job opportunities. The precise role will be dependent on the location and their requirements. Also, is it the ideal chance to interact with other individuals and be more engaged.

You can easily find work by inquiring at the location. Also, there are sites with a broad and their availability. You can even use this information as a guide and tailor your trips around available opportunities.

Search for Day Labor

Some locations employ day laborers; this applies to summer camps as well as many other locations. These jobs usually require a lot of physical prowess while others may need precise skills.

You can also look out for local postings or advertisements on websites like Craigslist. There are numerous staffing services that place emphasis on daily labor that can help you get work. You will go through a process of vetting, and it can take time to get accepted. Still, they offer you access to jobs you would not have found otherwise.

Engage in Odd Jobs or DIYs

If you do not want anything to do with an organization, you could try out DIY or odd jobs. There are always people that require work done and will search for people on Craigslist, local papers, or bulletin boards.

You can also make your adverts yourself. This is ideal if you are in the same location for a while. It can be a practical method to find work. It also means that you will often be doing various things which will ensure you don't get bored doing the same thing.

You could even go door to door and offer services like window cleaning, lawn mowing, and gardening, as long as you have the appropriate tools.

Work on a farm

There is an excellent program known as WWOOF USA which lets you work on a farm in exchange for a board and a room. The program keeps you occupied for half the day while you can do what you want with the rest of your time.

Technically, this is not a means of earning as you are not getting paid. However, you will be saving the cash required to park for a while. You also get the opportunity to sleep on a standard bed and take a bath or shower. If you have been on the road for a long time, you may have missed these sorts of luxuries.

Creating and Selling Crafts

Crafts are always in demand, and they can be an excellent means of earning. There are numerous ways of selling crafts online, but if you are on the road, selling physically may be a better option.

There are lots of ways to do this. For example, you may be able to locate local markets that let you set up a stall. Some people organizing yard sales may even give you a spot, especially if you offer something in return.

You will even see other individuals set up stalls by the roadside or sell from the back of their van. Just ensure you are not disobeying any local laws at any time.

Engage in Street Performance

This is a good idea for someone who has a bit of musical experience. The concept is to perform in busy locations for tips. Performing the right song in the right location can be profitable.

You will also have to go through the local regulations first. Some locations need you to be licensed, or there may be some limitations in the things you can do.

Performing is better in areas with lots of traffic. If you are going through remote areas, the audience may not be as much, which means your earnings will be lower.

Earn cash working as a courier

Since you are mostly going to be on the road, while not earn some cash at the same time? Websites like Roadie will offer you payments to make deliveries, and it allows you to choose the deliveries you find suitable.

The amount you earn on each delivery is dependent on the distance, and the amount is usually small, but you do have the possibility to earn a lot of cash for lengthier deliveries. You can also pick many deliveries all in the same direction to earn extra with little additional effort.

Payment goes into your bank account, and it takes between three to five days. Although you are not getting cash instantly, the system is great and it's a good idea to check it out.

Try Network Marketing

Network marketing companies are companies that let you earn cash by selling their products and developing a team.

This method is mostly used to earn cash in your environment. After all, the goal is to create connections and involve other individuals. Many of the companies have a catalog-based ordering system that would not be ideal on the road.

However, if you just wanted to emphasize on sales, inventory-based organizations are a better option, which are companies that let you purchase products in bulk at a cheap price. This way, you will have a range of products that you can sell from the back of a stall or a van.

Although it is not the most fantastic technique around, it is still a great choice. This is also a way to earn if you don't have an interest in developing your own products.

Try teaching locally

Teaching is an excellent method of earning some money, and this applies to a range of diverse talents. Think about some of your skills along with what individuals would like to learn.

You will be able to teach almost anything. However, when on the road, lessons that do not require many resources are great options. If you can teach outside, it's a better option. One of the best choices includes exercise classes. If the day out is lovely, people are likely to want to partake.

You can do adverts locally via signs or flyers. If you are in one location for a long period of time, you can also search local papers for listings.

Purchase and Resell items

The sale of items for cash while you are on the move can be tasking, but it offers you some distinct opportunities. You will be able to get access to a wide range of yard sales and markets. This will offer you the opportunity to locate more unusual and rare items that you could sell for a profit.

For this to work, you need to know what you are searching for and its value. For example, some individuals search for jewelry pieces they can sell as costume pieces. They then make a profit from the sale of gold. Others search for items with an underestimated value, like books or rare board games.

To sell, you will also need a location. Locating customers for rare products would be much harder than selling gold. You would probably need to depend on Amazon or eBay, which can be complicated if you are always on the move. Also, remember that you would require storage for anything you purchase, until you sell it.

This is a great method which can even be fun as you make cash in the process. Just ensure you plan properly, or you may end up with a lot of junk from your pocket.

Search for Temporary Jobs

Another great idea is to search for a traditional job that you can keep for a short period of time. This can include working in a retail store or waitressing. The concept is that you work for a while, save funds, then keep moving again. After this, you begin the process all over again in another city.

Doing this means your movement will be slower. You may even have to stay in one location for months depending on the sort of work you pick up. The significant part about this is that your traveling time will only be for traveling. You won't have to bother about working each day, and you will have to search for work at the next city you decide to stop at.

Renting Out your properties

If you have decided to live in an RV full time, there are perhaps a few things in your home that you have not sold yet and won't need anytime soon. So, why not make cash from them?

Home Rental

This is an effortless way to earn since you have no plans of using your home anytime soon. So, why leave it idle? The most popular method of doing this is via Airbnb, which has become quite popular over the last couple of years.

It is also required that you plan for the management of the area you wish to rent between one batch of renters and the next. Many companies can provide this service, and you can also place local adverts. A better option would be to hire someone who can effectively carry out this role. That way, you do not have to worry about much.

However, this earning method requires a little trust.

Rent out your Vehicle

There are also companies that give you the opportunity to rent out your vehicle. You may not get as much from this as you would from renting out your home, but it would not be as stressful either. Besides, if you have a vehicle you are not using, why not let it work for you?

This is not a quick way to earn, as you would need to wait until someone makes a booking. You may also want to emphasize long-term rentals as this means more cash and less hassle.

There are numerous services that could help you with this process. Some of these services also come with insurance plans to help keep your vehicle secure.

Making Money Online

Earning cash online is not easy while on the move, but achieving it is possible. There is also a range of approaches you can try out which offer you lots of flexibility.

The following are some of your best options:

Become a Travel Blogger

Travel blogging is a great fit for any individual who lives on the road. This offers you a great chance to speak about things you experience and get other individuals following. By doing this, you get to earn cash while on the road.

Attaining success in this area requires some planning. A broad range of travel blogs already exist, including in your area. You need to search for a distinct perspective or angle that can help you stand out.

One path to take would be to teach individuals how to effectively travel around the US, presuming this is what you are doing. For example, you could point out the sights which are popular, along with ways to save, as well as other useful information. Others have written about how you can earn while on the move, stating their personal experiences.

There are two core ways to make cash from travel blogging. One method is to host ads on your site, and the other is through affiliate marketing. These will earn you cash depending on the traffic on your website. You won't earn excessively, but the income can become reasonable if it adds up as the site becomes well-known.

Trade Stocks

If you have the background and skill, stock trading can be an excellent method of earning. The same applies to cryptocurrency. However, you must be cautious as losing money is quite easy, and lots of people frequently do.

This option is only a great idea for individuals who already have the skills and can afford to lose their investment. In this case, it may be a great option while on the road. For starters, it's best to go with something more reliable.

Sell your Pictures

It is recommended to take pictures while on the road. You are likely to find lots of fantastic places to take photos, so why not make some cash in the process?

One way is to sell your pictures professionally, like via your website. Some people have also created products using their pictures. One example is Canvas prints.

You can also utilize a print store to create cards based on your pictures and try selling them at markets. Regardless of the option you choose to go with, you have to be very efficient at marketing for this to work. Also, it's great to have unusual photos, as there are many amazing pictures and photographers already, so you want to stand out. This means that you will not earn anything from a picture of a sunset, regardless of how great it is, as there is intense competition in this area.

Another way is to sell stock photos, and the majority of the paid stock photo websites let you do this. The only problem with this is that you only make money if someone buys your picture. Normally, you won't get much from each sale. Also, if a few of your pictures get popular, it could be a great source of income.

However, note that being a little different helps, and no one will see your work if there are a host of other images that look like it.

Operate an Amazon FBA business

This is a system that lets you sell products on Amazon without the need to ship them manually each time you have a sale. Instead, Amazon stores your products in its warehouses. They take responsibility for a majority of processes which include packing and shipment of products to buyers.

This can be an excellent method to earn money, as long as you locate products people will buy. Achieving this requires planning and research, so starting up this business while you are on the road might not be too practical. There is a lot of work for you to do at the start, mainly because you have to deliver your items to Amazon. However, once you have begun, you will be able to keep it moving even when on the road.

Try Freelance Writing

This is something you would be able to do from any location. Freelance writing is quite a broad field. With lots of writers regularly earning income from what they do, the demand is also high. This means there is work available if you know where to search.

Websites like Freelancer and UpWork offer writers and freelancers a means of finding each other. You will also be able to advertise your job via a website. Also, you can write guest blogs and get paid for each article.

Like many other fields, it can be difficult to break into freelance writing. Many people believe they can write, so the competition is fierce. Also, some individuals who hire you will pay little while others will be fed up with writers performing poorly.

However, once you garner an excellent reputation and locate wonderful clients, freelance writing can be a great tool. For example, you could find a task that has to do with writing 100 small articles over a period of two months and sending them all in at once. You can easily do this on the road, especially with excellent internet connection for research purposes. Being familiar with the topic can also make things easier.

It may be a great idea to develop a client base and business before trying to earn on the move. Many regular clients may not be too bothered if you don't quickly reply to messages, but a new client may not get it.

Freelance Anything

Freelance writing is perhaps the less complicated kind of freelancing, solely because it doesn't require any unusual skills. However, if you do have other marketable skills, you may be able to earn from them as well. You can even make more, especially when it comes to specialized skills.

Websites like Fiverr and UpWork are great places to check out. The rule of thumb is that if you can do the work remotely, there is perhaps a market for it somewhere. In some situations, you will even be able to freelance in person. However, doing this may not be as easy, especially if you frequently have to be working with a new audience.

Regardless of the approach you decide to go with, creating your website is well worth it, as it offers you a base that you can use to promote yourself and highlight your skills. A website can be a place where you document things you are passionate about. Many people find that they end up amassing interest in their work as there is a growth in their audience. This remains the case even if the website does not relate to what they offer.

Do Remote Jobs

Many of the methods of earning while on the road focus on new types of jobs, along with side hustles. However, some individuals earn just by doing their regular jobs on the road. This is only applicable to jobs you can do remotely. Nonetheless, organizations are starting to get more flexible about people working remotely.

This is not exactly surprising, as the importance of many roles is the work that you are doing rather than where you are doing it from. For example, people in business can work remotely and hold conference calls when required. Also, teachers at college level can earn by teaching courses online. Many colleges now offer these courses, and they can quickly teach them remotely.

Affiliate Marketing.

This is another excellent way to earn, and you can do it from any location. All that's required is a functional laptop and access to the internet. The beauty of this is that regardless of where you go, your chance to earn does not change. It means you can channel your energy to other things.

The idea behind this is not difficult. You earn cash by promoting the products of other organizations and individuals. What this means is that you will be able to create affiliate links. When individuals click these links, it redirects them to the products. This does not mean the price changes for them in any way. However, for every purchase they make, you get a commission.

The commission is dependent on the actual program you are partaking in. In some situations, you may be earning around 10 percent. However, other programs offer more. If you can make substantial sales, the potential for earning is quite high.

If you can develop your own website, it can be easy to scale up affiliate marketing. It also makes it a fantastic long-term process. There are numerous ways to secure funds online.

Some are better than others, but they all have to do with exchanging hours for cash.

Developing your own affiliate website is one of the best ways to make money when you sleep and earn cash from any location in the world, even while on the road, as your website is active all year round, and you can access it from any smartphone or computer.

CHAPTER 7 - GUIDE TO LIVING COMFORTABLE IN AN RV

You now know how to make income while on the road, but you will also need to learn how to live comfortably in an RV. This means doing all the things that will offer you the utmost level of comfort while on the road.

This could range from keeping cool in your RV, eating healthily, and cleaning, among other things. The information in the upcoming chapter will serve you as a guide to help you through this process.

Now, read on to learn more.

Eating Healthily – How to Eat Healthily While on the Road

When living in an RV, it can be tasking to keep up with nutrition. It's tempting to consume meals from restaurants, fast foods and gas stations. There is also no space for refrigerators, small kitchens and you don't know if you will be using your appliances or not.

Eating healthily is crucial to those living in an RV full time, for many reasons. A balanced diet aids in averting and managing health issues like cholesterol, diabetes, and blood pressure.

Also, as a full-time RVer, you are probably going to be switching between sitting for long periods of time and being highly active when you get to a destination, with activities such as biking and hiking.

Having a balanced diet is crucial in order not to gain weight when you are not moving. This will ensure that you have the strength to explore when you get to new locations.

Other tips to eat healthily in an RV include:

Buy locally and seasonally

The healthiest and most sustainable diets consist majorly of lean meats, vegetables, fruits and grains along with a few goodies like snacks. It can be hard to cook perishables and store them, so it is crucial to purchase only what you know you can use and learn how to make raw meals.

Local farm stands, co-op grocery stores, and farmers markets are great locations to find fresh, cost-friendly ingredients. These will be the meals that contain the most nutrients you can find because they are usually organic and fresh.

In every state, there is a diverse range of products and a diverse range of stops. If you are traveling with a smartphone, there are also applications that can help locate the best local produce.

Ensure you always have healthy snacks available

If you are going to be on the move for a long period or if you are going to be shuffling between various destinations; having snacks close-by is crucial. You will need foods that can stay long periods without going bad, that you don't need to prepare, but that are still healthy.

Trail mix and nuts are great meals to benefit from while on the road. Head to a grocery store that has a section for bulk food, and you will be able to buy a mix of seeds, dried food, and nuts for a fantastic price.

Nutritional bars and protein bars can supply nutrients and keep you full, but make sure to check the labels and ingredients because some come loaded with as much as 400 calories and excess sugars.

Tuna or canned chicken can also be amazing for a quick salad, wrap or sandwich. Also, it can be stored for a long time. Fruits like oranges, apples, and pears are also ideal because you will also be able to store them for a long time. Also, you do not have to prepare or cook them.

Plan Ahead

In any healthy diet, planning is crucial. If you are going to be on the road full time, ensure to have enough snacks and food to see you through to your destination.

Also, planning when you are going to eat out and pre-selecting your options will let you make a more calculated decision about what you are going to consume and the cost.

Being adequately prepared will also provide you with more control over what you consume, and when you do choose to consume an exotic meal at a fancy restaurant, you will have more satisfaction because you will get precisely what you desire.

Having a balanced and healthy diet will let you thoroughly enjoy life. If you travel full time, it can be hard to stay away from restaurant meals and processed snacks, but you will be forced to eat healthy meals when you have them around and when you make plans for your special meals.

Exercising and staying fit

Working out and staying fit when RVing is crucial as it is easy to get lazy and add weight in all the wrong places. The tips below can help you exercise and remain fit.

Take Breaks

When going on long road trips, make a stop every 2 hours and be active for 10 – 15 minutes. Sitting for lengthy periods can cause damage to your body and result in all forms of negative health issues.

It's no secret that RVers enjoy driving. Staying behind the wheels for long distances through the fantastic countryside is terrific; however, you have to look out for the potential to get carried away and sit for too long at once.

Deep vein thrombosis is a very critical threat. Sitting for lengthy periods can result in blood clots in your legs. It is especially dangerous for those of a certain age and on specific medications. Tiredness can also be extremely dangerous when driving any vehicle. So, always ensure you take breaks.

Pull over, go outside and stretch. You can jog on the spot or do anything to get your blood flowing.

Take a Hike!

One of the best methods to stay in shape is probably by walking, especially if you are getting older and doing intensive interval workouts is not suitable for you.

Doctors recommend doing on average of 150 minutes of aerobic activity weekly as an adult. You can easily attain this by doing a quick walk every day. So, stretch your feet and shake off that lengthy drive.

Being on the road in an RV can offer you access to some fantastic nature reserves, national parks, and hiking trails. It would be a horrible idea not to combine exploration and exercise. Head out there and exploit the great outdoors while staying healthy.

Try Biking

This is a better option than walking, as cycling is one of the best methods for cardiovascular exercise. It is also amazing at keeping you healthy and fit while making sure you don't add excess weight.

The only downside is that you would certainly require a bike and a location to store it. However, most great RVs have lots of storage space or come with a mounted bike rack at the back.

If you do not have adequate space, you could even use a foldable version. Regardless of your choice, having access to a bike is an excellent method to keep fit and cover more ground when you decide to explore a new city.

Use Local or Campsite Facilities

The majority of the time, you will be residing in special RV campsites that offer services to such vehicles and their owners. Many will offer great facilities you can exploit. These could range from a tennis court to a well-equipped gym. Some of them also come with full-sized swimming pools and mini golf courts.

But, if you want to work out in a proper gym, you can look at the possibility of joining an international chain in order to be able to use their facilities in every location you visit.

Alternatively, many bigger towns come with a fitness center. It will allow you to utilize amazing facilities in any country you decide to visit or any location you choose to camp at for the night.

Watch your meals

Watch your diet. This is extremely crucial as what goes into your body is as crucial as your exercise routine. Stick with a healthy diet that consists of lots of fruits and vegetables. It might be difficult to resist the urge to head into diners and burger joints while on the road, but if you want to stay fit, you will want to resist the urge and keep moving.

Don't eat while driving. When you do this, you have a higher likelihood of overindulging due to sleepiness or boredom. Set a rule that you will only eat during driving breaks.

Plan your meals and snacks ahead. Ration your snacks so you have a lower probability of overeating. Bring lots of veggies, fresh fruits, nuts, and veggies. Having snacks close by will keep you away from junk food.

Engage in strength training exercises. If you don't engage in exercises that help in building strength, it may result in sarcopenia, which is natural muscle wasting that happens when we get older, and we all deal with it. The only way to battle this condition is with strength training.

Keeping Warm on The Road

When winter hits, you don't want to be caught unaware in your RV while on the road. Many RVers are literally left in the cold due to inadequate preparations.

RVs are not like your regular homes, so cold weather can be a severe problem if you don't prepare properly or know how to prevent the cold.

Thankfully, there are a few things you can do to keep you warm in your RV during these cold periods.

Service the Furnace

Before the cold weather begins, it is advisable to try out your furnace and take it for annual servicing. Observe the external vents for pests.

Make sure you fill up your propane tanks, and the selector valve is functional. Check all wirings to ensure they have not been chewed through by pest or mice.

Vacuum the Vents of your Furnace

This could be a part of servicing your furnace. Because these vents are situated on the floor, they can collect small stones, dust, hair ties, and pet hair, among other things.

Take off the vent cover, wash it using hot soapy water and allow to dry. Before it dries, use a vacuum to clear out the vents and ensure the hose gets as far as it can.

However, ensure you do not damage the metallic hose which goes to the furnace. When you are through, put the covers back, and you are good to go.

Utilize heat tape

If you have access to electricity, you can wrap your hoses using heat tapes to stop them from freezing.

Insulate your carport

You can insulate the carport of the RV using high-density foam and fiberglass. It is not appealing, but it helps to keep some of the cold out.

Having extra insulation is not a bad idea, especially during freezing temperatures. Although many campers come with insulation, factors like the model, make, and maintenance can affect it.

Also, ensure you insulate the hot water pipes. If you get cold, a warm bath can help you heat up. Also, if needed, make use of foam covers, old clothes or spray foams.

Use your Heat Pump

If you RC comes with a heat pump aside from your furnace, you can occasionally use it if the cold outside is extreme. Additionally, if you are connected to an electric pedestal, this will let you conserve your usage of propane.

The distinction between a heat pump and furnace is that the heat pump heats from the ceiling while a furnace heats from the floor. However, ensure you note the temperature outside before using it and follow the instructions from the manufacturers.

Use your Electric Fireplace

Many motorhomes, campers, and wheels are being fitted with exotic electric fireplaces. The majority of them even come with temperature control.

If you are connected to an electric pedestal, it is ideal to keep you warm without having to use the furnace. The only downside is that it can get costly if you are using metered electric pedestals.

Use your Window shades

Aside from privacy or making your camper dark during the day time, these also serve other functions. They can play the role of insulating barriers and help to keep some of the cold air from getting in. If you have them, there is no point leaving it idle, so use it to keep the cold out.

Leave your heater at a minimum of 50 degrees

It's never a great idea to turn off the heater. Set it to the lowest possible temperature to prevent things from getting frozen.

Leave your cupboards open

When it gets freezing outdoors, leave cabinets that would normally hide things like water tanks and plumbing open. You will need all the heat you can get, so be sure to leave all the right cupboards open so that the heat can get into the area.

Insulate air vents and windows

This is something you can try if you do not have a completely insulated carport. You can insulate the windows and add some insulation to your air vents. You can equally insulate walls, the roof, and the floor with heavy blankets.

Do not forget to air out your trailer

Moisture is a byproduct of propane. So, if you are using your heater but everything else is sealed, it will result in a lot of moisture accumulation. Heat can help dry out your trailer.

Dress warm

Although your RV has to be warm to avert freezing, an easy solution is to dress warm when the internal temperature of your RV is a little cold.

Keeping Your RV Cool

Similar to the excessively cold periods, hot days can equally be a challenge, and the A/C unit might not be adequate to keep you cool.

At times like these, a bit of creativity is essential.

Below are a few tips to help you stay cool in your RV.

Run your A/C Early

Even before it begins to get hot outside, turn on your AC, so it cools the floors, walls, and ceilings of your couch. Doing this is easier than trying to cool down a hot RV.

RV Orientation

This has to do with parking your RV. The direction it faces in relation to the sun has a lot of impact on the internal temperature. Park your RV close to a shady tree to minimize the effect of the sun.

Also, position your RV so the sun is shining on the side that has the lower number of windows. Noting these tips can help drastically reduce the level of heat that gets in your RV.

Close the windows

Huge picture windows bring in the highest amount of heat. Even with their mild tint, the internal temperature can drastically go up when the sun hits them.

To deal with this, try to lower the shades or cover windows using a reflective bubble known as Reflectix. You will be amazed at how it instantly drastically stops the transfer of heat.

Ventilation

Ensure that the RV has adequate ventilation. The major objective is to get warm air out and bring in fresh air. You can do this by opening windows on the side closer to shade and closing those on the side which is warmer or sunny.

Ceiling vent vans can be of great help when it has to do with moving air in the RV. There are numerous great brands that can help you move around lots of air.

Refrigerator Vent

The RV refrigerator lets out lots of heat as it cools food. The heat can get stuck in the RV and lead to excess warming. The majority of the units come with external vents on the roof or side of the RV to get rid of this heat.

Always ensure that the vent is not obstructed by debris. You can also fit in a fan in the fridge's ventilation area to get rid of more heat. Also, ensure you shade the fridge's external panel, so it functions more effectively and creates less heat.

Close the Shower Skylight

If your RV shower has a skylight, note that this can let in a lot of heat during sunny periods.

Avert this issue by removing the inner covering and switching it with Reflectix insulation. Alternatively, you can use Velcro tape to block the sun.

Have Tarps Handy

Always ensure you have a tarp, or even a couple in your RV, as they are extremely useful and offer immediate shade.

Attach a tarp close to a tree, and you have just made a cool location to relax.

Use LED lights

Halogen lamps or OEM are the standard lights that come in your RV. Although they function effectively, they let out a lot of heat in comparison to LED lights.

Simply swapping to LED lights can make a considerable difference in keeping you cool.

Do your cooking outside

Cooking generates heat. For this reason, it could be a bad idea to do it in your RV. You can use a grill or camp stove to make most of your meals.

Use the crock or Dutch oven rather than a hot oven so the heat stays outside.

Keeping Your RV Tidy

If you are living full time in an RV, it may be difficult to stay organized because of how limited space is. It may take some trial and error on your part, but below are some tips to keep it tidy and organized.

Try to place things in intuitive locations

Consider how you live in the RV. Ensure items that you make use of every day can be accessed with ease and are in a convenient location. Items that you use in the kitchen should be close to the kitchen.

Place things that you use outdoors close to the door. Don't be scared to change where you place things a few times. Finding locations that work may require some effort.

Search for organization tools after studying the trailer

As opposed to purchasing a load of items you may not need to keep your RV organized, it's best to be organized before purchasing items you require to complete the job.

You can first measure all the cupboards and cubbies in your RV, decide what you want to place there, then purchase bins designed for those locations, for example.

Clean up instantly

When living in a little space, it is crucial to clean up immediately. If you ignore cleaning up even once, you may later regret it. Clean up dishes the instant you are done eating. Make up your bed as soon as you get up and don't leave clothes you take off lying about.

When you are done using electronics, put away the chargers, so they do not add to the clutter. You will do various things in your RV so not cleaning it off instantly could result in a chain of organizational disasters.

Cooking – How to Cook Meals in an RV

When living in an RV, cooking your meals is important, as eating out and junk food is expensive and unhealthy. It's best to prepare your meals and fill them with the most nutritious ingredients you can find.

The tips below will help ensure cooking is easy:

Leave meals simple

Cooking meals that are simple will make things go a lot faster. If you try to cook creative and new meals every time, you will end up spending lots of energy. Also, you will be left with unused ingredients which may end up taking lots of space.

When you leave meals simple, you can cook them over and over with just a few ingredients.

Purchase some great cookware pieces for your RV

Even though picking entire cookware set for your RV may seem like a great idea, it is not a practical one. You do not have enough space to place all of those pans and pots, and you most likely don't have enough burners to utilize all of them anyway.

A better idea would be to purchase a huge six or eight-quart pot. The best option is cast iron steel, while stainless steel is also a good option. A huge crockpot is also an excellent option for cooking in your RV, but note that you will require a dependable source of electricity for no less than four hours to use it.

Make plans in advance

If you will be cooking in your RV for days, make plans to do all the slicing, chopping, cutting and rationing of ingredients in one go. Aside from saving you time, it will also help you save water because you won't need to wash as many knives and cutting boards every day.

To make things less complicated, you can purchase pre-prepped ingredients. The produce section in a majority of grocery stores has stuff like pre-washed greens and chopped vegetables.

Cook enough to last two meals

Make plans, store and consume leftovers. However, this may not be that easy if you have a lot of mouths to feed. But, if you are just one or two living in the RV, this is an excellent way to maximize time and have affordable and tasty meals when you are famished.

Try using Fire

Cooking in your RV does not mean you need to cook inside the RV. Instead, go out and prepare your meals using a grill. Also, a great option is to cook via a campfire.

Many RV parks come with grills and fire pits for guests, so you may not even have to come with yours. Also, when you cook meals outside, you don't need to make a lot of preparation for great meals.

There are a lot of options available in regards to the meals you can cook. Hot dogs, burgers, chicken as well as more comprehensive things like fish and steaks are great options on a grill.

You can wrap potatoes in foil, and you can brush veggies with a little oil and toss them on the grates. You can also thread them on bamboo skewers. If you feel like exploring, you can grill some fruits like slices of pineapple.

Nothing is more appealing than the taste of meals you cook over an open fire.

Remember to clean up

This is by far the worst part of cooking. However, whether in your home or your RV, it is still crucial. Allowing dirty dishes to gather in your little RV kitchen sink will attract insects, bad smells and discourage you from consuming meals in your vehicle.

If everyone gives a hand with the drying, washing, and cleaning up, things will go a lot quicker.

Dishware

If you enjoy cooking and staying in the kitchen, it may be difficult to live without your best dish selection and appliances for a while.

Keeping your RV tidy means you have to make do with as little as possible in your RV kitchen, so you need to let go of most things. The following tips can help with keeping things realistic in regards to dishware.

Allow each person one set of dishes

It would be very unrealistic to fill up your kitchen with every dishware you like. If you are traveling with a lot of people, plan on having two of each necessary utensils for everyone.

Only include the stuff you use daily

Only fill up your RV with stuff you use frequently. In most homes, kitchens are filled up with items we sometimes do not use for a long time. This won't work in an RV. Ensure you only have stuff you frequently use and later on, you can get rid of more things you find out you don't need.

Keeping the RV Clean

Being on the road full time, parking, driving in the dirt, and traveling through numerous weather conditions all have an effect on your RV. The cleaner you ensure your RV is, the easier it prevents the usual wear and tear that comes with being on the road all year round.

Your goal should be to wash the external part of your RV no less than once a quarter. It could be more, and this depends on how much time you spend traveling and where you go.

The following tips can help to keep your RV clean. They include:

Go through the Instruction Manual

The instruction manual is a bundle of information that can offer you tricks and tips to clean the interior and exterior of your RV. This consists of the kinds of cleaners you should use and those you shouldn't. It also contains instructions for specialized care.

You can also check out the website of your RV manufacturer to get additional tips to clean and make your RV shine. If you fail to go through the instruction manual, it could result in damage to the finishes and surfaces of your RV.

Let go of products with brand Names

The majority of RV materials don't differ from other kinds of living or vehicle materials. You may want to buy a solution made solely for RVs or a brand-name cleaner, but the reality is that lots of general and common household cleaners work just as well. These help in keeping your RV clean, and they include window cleaners, dish soap as well as distilled white vinegar.

Although those exotic products sold at the RV store seem fascinating, they are also more expensive.

Purchase a Quality Handheld Vacuum

The internal part of an RV consists of numerous nooks and crannies that can quickly gather dust, food debris and other items from your various adventures.

Purchasing a standard vacuum cleaner is not advised because it is too large for most RVs, so it's best to invest in a quality portable vacuum cleaner. Speak to other RVers and go through reviews to find what suits your RV best. Always search for a vacuum that comes with a hose attachment to get to the tiniest parts of your RV.

Clean Both Window Sides

Nobody wants the windows in their environment to be filled with grime and filth, so it's best to clean the internal and external parts of your windows to see things.

If your RV is not on the large side, you can do this by using any kind of window cleaner and a clean cloth. If your RV has numerous large windows, you may want to consider using an extendable squeegee. However, if you don't want to go through the stress, you can purchase a membership at the local carwash for oversized vehicles.

Remember your door and window seals

The door and window seals of your RV consist of rubber, which can gather dirt and dust. Clean your door and window seals frequently using gentle dish detergent. You can also use a specialized cleaner.

In this case, you may want to purchase a cleaner that also moisturizes seals aside from cleaning to help them last longer. This is very crucial if you are going through the arid American southwest that can dry out seals.

Flush those tanks

Your black and gray water tanks can cause lots of nasty odors. While these tanks don't have a direct impact on the appearance of your RV, a tank which isn't correctly maintained will make you uncomfortable while spending time outside or inside your ride.

Dump and flush your tanks as needed to ensure your entire ride is clean. Ensure you have a hose, a pair of standard powerful rubber gloves, a bucket, and other crucial items used to dump and clean your tanks.

Avert Mildew and Mold

These are the core enemies of most RVers, and they flourish in moisture, so minimize it in your RV. This consists of running your AC in humid areas, opening doors and windows when you can, and purchasing packets which help in absorbing moisture for storage areas and closets.

If you have a material that whiffs of mildew, stay away from detergent as it can help feed these critters.

Replace old propane tanks

Nothing can make your RV seem like an old tin can quicker than old propane tanks. If you always refill your tanks, you may want to replace them if they are damaged or repaint them if they are still in a fantastic condition. Just like painting the walls can quickly change the overall look of your home, the same goes for tanks.

Clean Those Tires

Tires make up a significant aspect of the external part of the RV and nothing makes it look more appealing than shiny, sleek, black tires. Many commercial tire cleaners work perfectly well for cleaning RV tires, but make sure you first go through customer reviews.

If you are driving a large rig, you can quicken the tire cleaning process by going to a car-wash for oversized vehicles.

Remember to clean the roof

It is crucial to clean your RV roof to avoid internal leaks and other problems. Lots of modern RV roofs are developed with membrane roofing, but you can still come across metal roofs.

If you have a metal roof, you can wash it the way you would the exterior part of the RV. But if your RV is developed with modern membrane roofing, it is ideal to use a specialized cleaner which you can get in camping and RV stores.

Cleaning a membrane roof twice a year is adequate to ensure it is in great shape. You can also take this moment to inspect the roof for any rips, tears, cracks and other damage.

Purchase Magic Erasers

Magic erasers can pick up stains and remove stains and dirt that even the strongest cleaners are unable to touch. Magic erasers are made of fine sandpaper, so be sure they don't cause damage to the materials or surfaces of your RV before you use them.

RV forums are great places to get advice and tips that you won't be able to find on the website of your RV manufacturer, such as using magic erasers for cleaning.

Clear Out Your Fridge

It is easy to abandon leftovers from the previous night in your RV back fridge, but smelly items can make the small RV space smell bad. Be careful about what you place in the fridge of your RV and frequently clean out the contents.

It is very easy to forget things that can go bad in the fridge of your RV, so always keep this in mind.

Carry Out Routine Maintenance

An RV which is not adequately maintained has more likelihood of giving you issues with cleanliness. Loose oil, smoky exhaust and other nasty things that occur when you neglect your RV can give the side of your vehicle an awful color.

By correctly maintaining the inner parts of your RV, you can minimize very bad smoky smells that clog the air around you and the exterior of your RV.

Freshen up your linens and mattresses

When you are out on the road, it is easy to go for a long time without remembering to change your mattress and linen. These unkempt linings can make you feel grimy and can fill up with dead skin cells and sweat.

It's advised to always travel with two linen sets so you can change your sheets on the go. If your mattress has a musty smell, take the sheets off, spray the mattress with a combination of lavender, water, and essential oils and let the mattress air out for a while.

Have a doormat to collect dirt

This is a great way to keep the inside of your RV neat. Place a doormat at the RV deck or trailer entrance. You can knock the dust off your shoes before going in and get any guests to do same too.

An excellent method of cleaning is to prevent things from getting dirty initially.

CHAPTER 8:
LIFE ON THE ROAD AND MUST VISIT DESTINATIONS FOR US RV TRAVELERS

In this chapter, I will be telling you about life on the road and some crucial information you should know to make your life on the road easier.

First, let's take a look at how to distinguish between RV parks, Trailer parks, and Campgrounds.

RV parks, Campgrounds, and Trailer Parks; How are they different?

There are a couple of terms associated with RVs such as RV resorts, RV Parks and campgrounds. While different, these terms sound quite similar. There aren't any hard-set definitions, even on the internet.

But in the RV world, sites named as parks typically offer full RV hookups, as they tend to offer amenities solely for trailer and RV owners, even going to the lengths of banning tents. These sites typically have activities catered to adults and kids.

A campground is extremely rustic and has tenting as the major accommodation option. It is extremely family oriented, with numerous activities that are sure to be fun for the kids.

Sites like these are typically filled up to the brim during weekends and holiday periods. The people at campgrounds usually love the outdoors, especially given the fact that they are bound to be living and sleeping underneath the stars. These sites are typically rowdy during the weekend as almost all of the activities are outside. State parks can also be classified as campgrounds.

A site named as a trailer park is either a permanent or temporary area for travel trailers and mobile homes. Pros associated with these sites are low housing costs, as well as fast and rapid transportation of the unit from one area to another, like if you had to move for a job while keeping the same house. Trailer parks have been stereotyped, particularly in popular American culture, as housing for people of lower income, with most occupants living either below or at the poverty line whilst having almost no social status and living a lifestyle that is both desultory and deleterious.

Free RV Campgrounds and Camping

RV parking refers to a site that allows RV users to stay the night, while RV camping enables users to stay multiple days in an RV.

Free RV parking areas can be found anywhere on private and public property. A quick internet search will come up with dozens of websites that have been devoted to finding and listing free parking locations for RVs.

You will be able to find free RV camping sites on both private property and public lands. Also, certain timber companies enable free camping on their land. The bulk of free RV camping sites can be located on public property. Asking the local sheriff or police office for sites that allow free parking for RVs is the best way to go. All it takes is a phone call to get more information. RV travelers on the eastern seaboard are likely to find a lack of free RV parking sites as land is extensively privately owned.

It is imperative to note the vehicle when setting out for remote areas. This is particularly helpful as locating free RV camping sites is easier if the RV is smaller.

How to Locate Amazing Free RV Camping Sites

Locating free camping sites for RVs tends to become seamless once you have more experience. The simple truth is that great RV camping sites that are free can't be found without the help of a map. If you have no map, the next best thing is to get someone that knows the location to get extremely accurate directions. There are numerous maps available that list wonderful free camping sites. In a move to keep with the times, electronic navigation can also help find places, as well as provide topographic information coordinated by GPS. This is a piece of great equipment suitable for even the most adventurous RV camper.

Ideas for Free RV Camping

If you are searching for free RV camping sites, you will be pleased to know that public lands all over the western part of the USA and certain parts of eastern USA allow free RV camping. Certain states enable either low cost or free RV camping on the bulk of public properties. Arizona, for example, requires RV users to purchase a $20 public lands recreation permit which grants unfettered camping access on state lands. Colorado, on the other hand, has a couple of owned and leased lands which allow RV camping at no charge. It is recommended to check the public lands section of state government sites for more information.

There is a plethora of places to consider when searching for RV parking or camping locations at no cost. However, it is recommended to seek permission to park overnight. Once again, the size of the RV matters when searching for free spots that don't require authorization. Think the smaller, the better.

Below are a couple of sites to check out:

- Truck Stops are a great site as seeking permission isn't usually a requirement. It is imperative to consider the trucks should you choose to park here.

- Nightclubs and Grain elevators are great sites, but it is best to seek permission so your RV does not get in the way.

- Supermarkets are a great site. However, not all cities allow RV parking for the night.

- Certain fraternal organizations might offer no-cost RV camping. Fairgrounds and parks owned by any level of government might allow RVs to camp overnight when those sites are not being used. Churches are also great sites. However, it is best to seek permission and make reservations by calling ahead.

- Hotel parking lots, as well as truck terminals, are some other great sites to get free parking for your

RVs. However, it is imperative that you get permission. As stated earlier, there are quite a few RV parking and camping possibilities. It is best to keep a low profile if you are unable to get explicit permission or if you would rather not ask. If the RV comes with extra features such as TV antennas, jacks, and slide outs, it is best not to use them as they could draw attention to you.

- There are websites that provide links to information on public land and to numerous free RV parking and camping sites. The best RV camping spots are usually ones located on public land. However, this information requires quite a bit of research, especially if the areas in question are far from familiar territory.

Maintaining your RV – Why you should create a monthly checklist

There are numerous positives to developing and sticking to a prompt RV maintenance routine. Apart from making the RV safer and nicer, it also extends its usage life while lowering repair costs which in turn result in the RV getting a better resale value.

There is so much you can gain from having a maintenance culture, which is why every RV owner should adhere to this.

Develop a schedule

An effective RV maintenance structure requires a couple of things:

- A date planner to clearly mark out the days maintenance is scheduled
- An itinerary of things that need to be done on those specific dates.

Making use of an electronic calendar helps as you can set up recurring events, whilst also including specifics regarding maintenance. Varying maintenance activities are to be done using an interval system.

The engines powering RVs are also to be scheduled for maintenance; however, instead of the intervals being based on time, they become mileage based.

Keeping Records

You should keep a logbook of every maintenance activity you carry out, especially if the activities deal with the overall safety or integrity of the RV. It is recommended that these activity records are kept safe, perhaps where the complete maintenance checklists are kept.

It is important to date the entries, as well as note the dates when the accompanying checks were carried out, as well as the resulting diagnosis, replacements or repairs. The logbook is irretrievable proof of the check listed tasks you complete.

Certain RV insurance providers request to see evidence of maintenance.

Should you decide to rent out your RV, renters can be assured to know that a logbook of maintenance is kept.

A maintenance log can aid in reassuring guests who rent your RV. It is also great for when you need to sell the RV as it increases its value.

Quarterly checklist for maintenance – What should it Entail?

It is imperative to note that every RV is unique. Try to consult the owner's manual to get recommended maintenance guidelines.

Electrical System

A basic electrical systems safety test requires that you connect the RV to the mains. Begin by checking the circuit breaker and ensuring every one of the fuses are connected and in good working order.

The next is to solely test every light, appliance and electrical outlet in the RV. If one isn't working, there might be an electrical fault of some sort. Should the furnace or stove have an electric starter, it is best to check it as well. Last but not least, the battery voltage should be checked to ensure proper charging.

Propane System

If propane is used, it is imperative to have a system that can detect propane leaks. The sensor is typically situated closer to the floor since propane tends to sink as it is denser than air.

Begin by ensuring the detector is turned on by making use of the inbuilt test feature. To check for leaks, you need to the main valve and the windows while doors are closed. Leave it for two hours, and if the alarm goes off, then there is a leak somewhere which you have to fix as soon as possible.

Appliances

At every quarter interval, you need to carry out a visual and fictional inspection of major appliances. Turn on the burners on the stove, use the microwave, check the temperature of the fridge, etc.

You need to clean every one of these appliances and note unusual noises during operation. If you observe any fault, it is important to deal with it as soon as possible.

Brakes

You need to inspect your brakes visually. If you have no prior knowledge on brakes, you should begin by finding out what kind of brakes the RV has and what signs to watch out for during an inspection. The most widespread issue is typically wear and tear on brake pads.

To get a better feel for problems, it is also advisable to conduct a live brake test. If the RV in question is a trailer, it is imperative to clear the brake connector with an application of contact cleaner. At this time, you need to inspect the breakaway switch.

Lubricate locks and hinges

A three months interval is frequent enough to lubricate the locks and hinges on the RV. Typical household oils work great for the hinges. It is best not to apply too much, and the excess should always be wiped away to prevent causing spillage and streaks.

The locks are to be lubricated using lubricant based on dry graphite. Try making a small checklist of all the hinges present in the RV, as it is quite easy to forget a couple of hinges, especially if they are on less frequently used doors.

Lug Nuts

It is important to know the correct torque rating on all the lug nuts present on the wheels of the RV, as it helps to put this information in your checklist.

You can use a hydraulic or mechanical torsion wrench to get the most accurate torque for every lug nut. The best method to do this is by lifting the wheel off the floor.

Power Wash

If the aim is to rent out your RV, it is important that it looks clean when it is about to be picked up. It is ideal that you properly wash the RV's exterior every quarter. It also helps to apply wax or any form of treatment recommended by the manufacturer.

You have to wash the undercarriage thoroughly as well as the roof and the wheels. Dirt in previously listed places tends to stick around, thereby corroding the RV.

Mileage Check

You need to carry out a quarterly mileage check on the RV if you don't use it much. Usually, the RV's brakes and engine have quite a couple different service recommendations.

The best way to maximize the use of the RV is to strictly follow the recommendations listed by the manufacturers.

Tires

Before making any trips with the RV, you need to check the tires. The frequency of these tire checks is the reason why they do not appear on the quarterly list.

Nevertheless, the requirement to ensure there is only a 50% maximum on tread wear during every inspection is significant, and tire pressure should also be checked to ensure that it is the exact figure given by the RV manufacturer.

RV Memberships and Clubs

Clubs and memberships for RVs have been in existence since the initial RV was launched at Madison Square Garden back in 1910. The years following its debut, several RVs were dispersed in a vast array of routes due to their different features and benefits. Every RV club occupies a unique niche, offering a community for fellow RV owners. Every single one of them requires an annual fee to get discounted rates.

The majority of the older RV clubs are not in existence anymore. The ones that do remain have to compete with many new startups. There are a couple of questions to consider when attempting to differentiate between the plethora of choices available. Does the club reflect quality? Are newer organizations able to compete with already established ones? What are the fees and how frequently are they due? Are there discounts available and if there are, are they the type that people want?

Below, I will be providing answers to all the questions above. Additionally, it helps to shed light on precisely why some RV clubs are different from others.

Which RV Club is right for you?

You will be able to answer this question after taking into account your residence, travel frequency, and budget costs

Costs typically vary from as little as $30 each year, with the benefits received ranging in accordance to price. There are clubs that cater to pros and amateurs, full-timers and renters, as well as glampers and boondockers.

Certain clubs have many benefits, whilst some offerings barely scratch the surface. When selecting the RV clubs to enlist in, it helps to categorize them.

Clubs fall into three categories. They are:

- Affiliate based
- Specialty RV clubs
- Brand Specific Clubs

Affiliate-Based RV Clubs

Affiliate-based RV clubs are typically clubs that offer reduced camping prices on all affiliated parks located all over the United States. These are usually the most widespread of RV clubs.

Brand Specific RV Clubs

These clubs typically give you discounts on certain RV park chains. This does mean a reduction in variety; however, members can be sure of what they are getting.

Specialty RV Clubs

These RV clubs typically differ from the widespread models listed above, as these tend to offer different methods to help save money.

Places you must check out if you are in the US

If you are RVing in the US and you want to witness fantastic destinations and scenic roads all within a couple of days, you should consider the following destinations.

These sorts of trips are great for those that rent RVs as they can go on their adventure and return the RV on Monday.

Hermann Wine Trail

This trip is one that is extremely short and has been ranked as one of the best road trip routes in the US. It provides plenty of time to see the sights, tastes, and smells associated with the wine country of Missouri while tracing the parallel route of the Missouri River for over 20 miles.

Whilst this trip is short, there are many things to do along the Hermann Wine Trail. There are numerous wineries, as well as a number of monthly events available. This is a great way to remain occupied for the duration of your trip.

The Florida Keys

The Florida Keys are a perfect destination if you want your road trip to have a tropical feel. The Florida overseas highway spans from the entirety of the keys, from Key West to Key Largo, with about 100 miles of wonderful tropical road.

There are numerous activities all along this tropical route, with some of the popular ones being snorkeling, exploring state parks, visiting museums, and swimming with wildlife.

There is no doubt that the overseas highway is a very scenic route that could possibly be one of the very best road trip routes in the United States.

The Alabama Coast

Alabama's Gulf Coast has a couple of historic sites available in the United States. Visitors to this route can view mansions and the magnificent gardens they contain, as well as have a look at World War II submarines and battleships.

You will be able to take on a cultural journey along the Alabama Coastal Connection, with a rich and fascinating landscape full of Spanish, French and Creole influences.

You can start the journey in Mobile Alabama towards the south using Route 98.

Cherohala Skyway

This amazing road trip route takes you through the mountains and plains of North Carolina and Tennessee.

The Cherohala Skyway spans 40 miles and starts in Southeast Tennessee in Tellico Plains. In the beginning, visitors can explore the numerous rivers and overlooks found on the Skyway.

Visitors to this scenic route can traverse through the Great Smoky Mountains, a location with countless historical and hiking landmarks.

The trip culminates at Robbinsville, North Carolina which houses the Joyce Kilmer Memorial Forest.

Death Valley

Death Valley is a road trip that you can't leave out when you mention a list of the best road trip routes in the United States.

The route goes from the largest tree in the world to the lowest and hottest place this part of the world. Certainly a place of extremes, Death Valley earns its name.

There is quite a large amount of area to explore, however, a trip scheduled for the weekend should take about 7 hours from Los Angeles via Death Valley to Las Vegas.

It is imperative to undergo proper planning, as well as research the climate before embarking on a trip, as temperatures of almost 134F have been observed in that area.

Must Visit Destinations for US Travelers: Longer RV Road Trips

This sort of trips is perfect for those that have a bit more time and want to go on a trip that offers them a longer adventure.

If you already have an RV, all you have to do is start packing and planning your route.

The following are the top places you need to check out:

Route 66

Possibly the most famous road trip in the world, Route 66 is the flagship of US road trips. It begins in Chicago, Illinois and ends in Los Angeles, California.

This road trip spans about 2,448 miles and gives you a deep peek into the evolutionary chart of American culture. The route includes Josie's numerous cities, expansive landscapes and small towns that you can explore.

The Pacific Coast Highway

The Pacific Coast Highway is another historical adventure.

When you head to this destination, you experience the ocean breeze on the coastal highway that spans the distance of Olympia, Washington to Los Angeles, California.

The highway has numerous attractions alongside it, with many famous towns and cities available for visits, as well as the fantastic sweeping vistas the United States can offer.

This is a great road trip for those that love the forest and the sea equally.

Cross-Country Trip: historical US-80

One of the most significant ways to explore the United States is to examine different sections of it. This road trip route offers the opportunity to travel all over the south.

The US 80 is an old highway and what remains of it will take visitors from San Diego, California to Savannah, Georgia. This route spans various diverse landscapes such as bayous, plains, and deserts.

Cuisine and culture are also diverse on this historic road. There are cuisines for everyone, from Tex-Mex to crawfish and barbecue.

Cross-Country Trip: The Great Northern

This road trip route is perfect for those that want to explore sections of the United States but that would rather not suffer the humidity associated with the south. The Great Northern road trip travels on the US 2 Highway.

The highway measures over 2,500 miles from Maine to Washington. This road trip is one of the longest road trips to take in the United States. Its length enables visitors to experience the beautiful mountains, prairies and hardwood forests.

The Great Northern is a road trip that would appeal to those that love nature, as there are numerous amazing vistas which are more prevalent than cities and towns. Visitors will appreciate this route as it gives them time to experience northern America's natural beauty.

CONCLUSION

The RV lifestyle is many peoples' dream. In the past, people usually waited until they were retired and had the funds and time to travel around the nation. Now, lots of individuals from various age groups want to live in a much more straightforward manner and make the time to enjoy traveling now that they still have the desire and energy.

I congratulate you on deciding to be one of the people who has chosen to become a part of the RV lifestyle. I advise you to keep this book close-by while on the road. Read it continuously and refer to the steps in the book if you ever get stuck.

At times, RVing full-time and staying in an unknown location scares off many people. Also, the idea of being out of contact with the world is also scary, and this makes them let go of the idea entirely.

However, this is not the case as RVing is quite flexible. You will be able to go to any location, anytime, anywhere, and for any reason. The world is yours to explore and nothing is holding you back. Do not be afraid to explore and be ready to go through a few setbacks along the line till you fully begin to grasp the concept of full-time RVing.

As you must have noticed while reading this book, it can help make your dream a reality. If the RV lifestyle is what you are after, then take the necessary steps and go for it. At first, it can be scary, but if you know what you are doing and follow the steps in this book, then it is undoubtedly a fantastic experience.

So why wait? Take the steps to begin right now.

www.ingramcontent.com/pod-product-compliance
Lightning Source LLC
Chambersburg PA
CBHW031154020426
42333CB00013B/652